PRAISE FOR
AFTER THE FLOWERS DIE

"Renee Leonard Kennedy is one of the most genuine and encouraging people I know. And those are exactly the qualities you want in an author of a book like this one. Renee has the voice and experience that qualify her to write on these difficult topics. I'm so glad that she wrote *After the Flowers Die*."

—JORDAN RAYNOR, national bestselling author of *Redeeming Your Time*

"Full of important information relating to legacy and estate planning for those navigating the complex world of loss and inheritance, *After the Flowers Die* is lovingly written for the grieving."

—ANDREW L. HOWELL, ESQ., co-author of *Entrusted: Building a Legacy That Lasts*

"We have all experienced different aspects of grief. The challenge is trying to navigate through the stages without feeling overwhelmed and lost. *After the Flowers Die* includes enough rawness to help readers navigate through the stages of grief gently. The book's Ponder Points provides a safe place for the reader to pause and process what has occurred, as well as plan for their own generational legacies. This is a practical guide for anyone who is going through loss regardless of how recent. It's comforting to find a book that validates the hard questions and emotions. This is a must for any counseling center wanting to help their clients work through the stages of grief."

—MICHELLE B. GALLIMORE, MS, MTS, LCMHC, CSAT, Clinical Director of The Oaks Therapeutic Community, The Oaks (theoakscommunity.org)

"As a pastor, I have frequently walked families through the many-faceted effects death brings when it visits. Death is an often frightening inescapable reality that causes many of us to avoid preparing for it. Yet, having watched more than a few individuals and families prepare well for death, I can't speak loudly enough about the importance of being ready for your own passing or the passing of your loved ones. *After the Flowers Die* invites you to do just that with winsome, introspective honesty about death and all of its dominoes. With the heart of a daughter, the love of a mother, the skill of a writer, and the savvy of a entrepreneur, she walks you through the varying consequences and spectrum of emotions when death visits. Read this book for yourself. And buy a copy for a loved one."

—DR. ROBERT HEFNER, Sr. Pastor, Pleasant Garden Baptist Church, Pleasant Garden, North Carolina

"In this gripping look at all that is involved when we experience the death of someone close to us, *After the Flowers Die* confronts and deals with an area Americans—and most Westerners—do not handle well: the loss of a loved one. For most of us, death is often sanitized and compartmentalized. We don't like the rawness and finality of it, and are unsure what to do. Using narrative style and vignettes from actual life experiences, Renee Leonard Kennedy journeys through the emotions and challenges we must deal with when we lose someone we love, and what it takes to move forward in our lives. The value in reading this book is not just for those having experienced recent loss. A very thought-provoking book, *After the Flowers Die* has lessons for us all, wherever we may be in our personal pilgrimages."

—DAVID LAWRENCE, Founder of the multi-weekly Healthy Faith Chats on Twitter at #HealthyFaith, social media professional.

"Death is both heartbreaking and backbreaking. The weight of sorrow meets the weight of responsibility. *After the Flowers Die* meets both these challenges head on, from a place of experience, through the lens of mourning. Renee Leonard Kennedy becomes that friend that mourns with you and that help that actually helps. Read the book and learn to do the same."

—R.C. SPROUL, JR.

"When my amazing Grandma passed away, I watched my mom and her siblings handle a mountain of to-do's while working through their own grief. I wish we'd had *After the Flowers Die* as a guide during that time. In its pages, Renee Leonard Kennedy offers practical guidance mixed with empathic support to help friends and family honor their loved ones last wishes…along with a head's up on the things that we don't know that we don't know. *After the Flowers Die* is a book that should be in every church library, bookshelf, estate planning resource, and as part of every household so it will be there when you need it."

—BETHANY JETT, award-winning author

AFTER THE FLOWERS DIE

Encouragement for
Walking Through Life
After Loss

RENEE LEONARD KENNEDY

After the Flowers Die

End Game Press books may be purchased in bulk at special discounts for sales promotion, corporate gifts, ministry, fund-raising, or educational purposes. Special editions can also be created to specifications. For details, contact Special Sales Dept., End Game Press, P.O. Box 206, Nesbit, MS 38651 or info@endgamepress.com.

Visit our website at www.endgamepress.com

Library of Congress Control Number: 2022932627
ISBN: 978-1-63797-047-8
eBook ISBN: 978-1-63797-046-1

Cover Design by Bruce Gore, Gore Studio Inc.
Interior design by Monica Thomas for TLC Book Design, *TLCBookDesign.com*
Cover image by Ilona Ilyés / Pixabay; Interior images from Adobestock.com

Printed in India
TPL
10 9 8 7 6 5 4 3 2 1

For my brothers and sister,
Roger, Robin and Russell,
And our parents,
Frank and Jackie*

*kids, see the acknowledgments

Table of Contents

AFTER THE FLOWERS DIE

It all began with grandmothers, as many thoughts do.

Mamaw and Nannie would tell me stories of my ancestors, stretching my knowledge from three generations to six, from seventy years to almost two hundred. Great-great aunts and uncles became more than names as my grandmothers told how their relatives had lived and died. Inevitably, the inheritances—material and immaterial—were spoken of, be they items, land, businesses, even sins.

When I was in my teens, Nannie and I longed to recreate her front-yard picnics, like the ones attended when I was a toddler hopping on Great Uncle Joe's lap. He named me "Sparkle Plenty," a name my mom reminded me of until her death in 2018. My grandmother and I would be thick as thieves, as my mom would say, sorting through picnic details.

Mental lists of cousins, aunts, and uncles were made. As was the menu—complete with Nannie's rolls and coconut cake, both from-scratch recipes created by handfuls and pinches of this and that. Tables would be loaded with food dishes and cast iron, old wooden chairs gathered from the barn, and a long, languid Sunday afternoon spent under the twin maples. This picnic went unrealized as my grandmother passed into history.

My ancestors' stories had impressed upon me the seasons of life, from beginning to end. From the death of a favorite cousin in my tweens to my grandparents and all those in between, I pondered the events happening to those left behind. Even now, I recall a young man in college I barely knew seeking me out for help. "My mom died. She left me two hundred and fifty thousand dollars. I need to do something. Buy a house, maybe?"

As a student of all things Forbes, who was simultaneously flunking out of school, I advised against that, since he was only twenty and newly grieving. I suggested waiting and investing at a later time. After having lived my parents' dream of building a fine family business, I knew enough to say, "But talk to professionals." Probably the only wise statement made in my early twenties.

Having talked about all the major passings with counselors, I used poetry and writing as a form of processing further. Since my late twenties, my initial thoughts on any financial or personal moves are the possible effects on my next generation. To the point, my adult son said, "Mom, you're obsessed with death." A friend echoed, "You talk a lot about death."

"When I lay these questions before God I get no answer. But a rather special sort of 'No answer.'
It is not the locked door.
It is more like a silent, certainly not uncompassionate, gaze. As though He shook His head not in refusal but waiving the question. Like, 'Peace, child; you don't understand.'"

~ CS Lewis, *A Grief Observed*

It took writing this book to see I wasn't preoccupied with death, as much as I was with the stories and lessons learned from the ones left behind.

The years flew by with many losses until 2016 came with a fury. A group of friends I'd known for many years and I experienced the deaths of our mothers or fathers. Every one of us, like dominoes falling, lost a parent, with one couple, fathers on both sides. We capped that tragic year off with a friend's father passing December 29, signaling the end of the hardest time in our collective lives.

We went from funeral to funeral, wondering what we were supposed to do after the flowers die, shellshocked by paperwork and varying amounts of will execution and inheritances. How do we handle this? Why didn't someone tell us? The people issues, the surprises that came afterwards, the inheritances that weren't money always rocked us the most.

Thus, these stories are personal, yet broad enough for your own application. If you are given to reading a book straight through, do so. Or skim through the chapter titles and see what catches your eye. The short chapters end with a Ponder Point that may or may not become an action taken today or in a year. Sometimes, the Ponder Point is subtle or in one case, non-existent. Some stories have no easy steps to take.

My hope is you find this wee book a comfort, a springboard to reflect, a reason to pause in between the paperwork must-dos of losing a loved one. I aspire to give you a heads-up on some unexpected acts that might arise, not covered in the realm of the professionals in an email or meeting. In the end, we enter in the deep of the following months after the flowers die and notice we have more in common than not. Confusion, sadness, and fear tend to solidify us.

May you see your loss journey like my grandmothers did. A painful passing, yes, but one day, a life story to be handed down to the next generation, which will touch the proceeding three. Through our struggles and pain, much is to be gained in the telling of how we moved forward, not just for our sakes, but for those yet to come. After all, love and legacy are the best of what we leave.

May mercy, peace, and love be multiplied to you.

RECEIVING

Accepting a gift bag fluffed with tissue paper is relatively easy. The biggest concern is whether our response will convey the proper appreciation to the giver.

Accepting the inheritance of cash or investments, however, is a different matter altogether. And whether that inheritance is a crumbling house or mansion, costume jewelry or diamonds, updated furniture or the duct-taped recliner, challenges exist in receiving this gift, even a lifetime of presents cannot prepare us for.

The response of an inheritance is as varied as people's personalities. Some react with ease, one lawyer said. For others, heartache engulfs us. We grieve as if receiving an inheritance—small, medium, or large—is a walk to the gallows of repeating our loved one's death. Others clothe themselves in panic, fear, and guilt. Feelings of being undeserving can arise, sure as sugar, as we have not earned any of this. Yet because we are gifted, we muster up a sense of duty or acceptance, if we can, while hiding the angst that couples the seemingly exchange of a material object for our loved one.

Then, other emotions arise while receiving assets.

Most of us have heard stories of a child being left out of a cash inheritance, or unequally gifted. A friend of mine has walked a similar story, but on the other side of the will. His mother left him all the silver, a higher percentage of stocks and cash, while his siblings received pottery, coasters, and wicker baskets. To add to the family dynamics, my friend had been named by his mother as sole executor of an extremely precise will.

This man had to not only receive more, but execute the gifting in accordance with the will. Not a greedy person, he said, "I don't know how many times I had to say, 'Mom's will states....'"

My parents took a more equalized approach. Being the black sheep of the family, I was surprised to be included in the will after the grief I'd given them during my wild decades. But include me, they did. It overwhelmed, both dealing with their deaths within two years, and receiving assets. We could barely catch our breaths, my sister and I repeated to each other. The stuff of inheritance was not the wrapped presents of Christmas or even the birthday check, but a physical memorial that screamed, "We, your parents, are now gone. Here is your portion."

It took me months of vein-pressuring stress and many "help me, Lords" to learn

"He did not know how long he sat there or what was happening to him, but at last he moved as if he were awakening and he got up slowly and stood on the moss carpet, drawing a long, deep, soft breath and wondering at himself. Something seemed to have been unbound and released in him, very quietly."

~ Frances Hodgson Burnett, *The Secret Garden*

these gifts are not just from my loved ones, but as my faith teaches, from the very God who knows me like no other. The words "Gratitude" and "Thanksgiving" had at last pierced my fog and fret. Although my fears were not eliminated, the guilt of inheriting was. All I had to do at that moment was receive, as I did each morning the sunrise, or lack thereof.

On the flip side, I had to wrestle with the bad gifts wrapped up in inheritance, often ranging from difficult situations to learning of horrific acts. The juxtaposition between the good gift and the bad is so vast, no easy answers can set any of this aright. The best we can do is link arms together and acknowledge some gifts are sunrises, and other are hardships, if not downright hellholes. Inheritance is layered with both, as life and death are common to us all.

Ponder Point As simple as it sounds, we walk the struggle of the same roads, just different scenarios. We are equalized by our journeys down the aisle in funeral homes or houses of worship, and our gatherings on mountaintops, coffee shops, or restaurants. We can relate to the loss of loved ones, and the act of receiving and often, the hardships of evil.

Somewhere in the mire, in our own timing, we venture forward. We are pushed by paperwork, but in the receiving, we are held by our emotions. In your timing, moving forward is the goal. This is the act of inheritance.

BLESSINGS

My daughter inherited a tin coffee can brimming with old pennies to sort through. My mother was convinced a wheat penny, worth a million dollars, was hidden in there, and she decided that this grandchild should have it. Periodically, my daughter would pour out the coins, searching for the elusive, expensive one. At last, she found a beat-up, aged penny.

"What am I supposed to do with this, Mom?" She showed me the prospective million-dollar coin. This being in the time before the internet, I said what mothers around the country have said for years. "Go to the library and get a book."

As a daughter who had a definite reading stack, she did what she thought best. She swept up all the coins and canned them, where they await discovery to this day.

Learning to receive is one work of inheriting. Taking possession of the blessing is another thing entirely. Often, an itchy, scratchy, unnamed emotion settles in. What do we do with these things? The question asked by my daughter was a good one. Blessings, as it turns out, are weighty baggage. Not only are we processing the loss of a loved one, but now we are processing a gift, either material or immaterial. A thing in exchange for a life does not seem like a fair trade or one most of us would rather not contemplate at this time.

Here we are, though, with the metaphorical coffee can of pennies in hand. I learned a lot by watching my daughter with this simple blessing. First, she put the gift on a shelf. For us, this looks like processing the emotions we are experiencing from the loss and gaining the blessing. Sometimes, this means not doing anything with the money, cars, houses, or collection of beer steins. Second, we examine the blessing. We ask questions of it. What exactly am I supposed to do with this? What might be the best course of action?

After we've made peace with our new life going forward, then, armed with the best advisors and libraries possible, we determine a course of action, from mink coats in the parents' closet to acreage in the country to the most precious of gifts—a moral code.

Blessings can pivot our habits, starting a new day out of debt, with a new way of handling material assets, a new view on how we might live our lives, affecting generations to come. Although our lives can use a boost of cash and cars, try to keep in mind the bigger picture. Leaving a legacy of morality outlasts all the material possessions in the world.

Ponder Point After a passing, a swarm of professionals and friends might have many suggestions on how to turn meager or large portions into greater assets. My friend, Luke, who recently retired from a successful funeral services business, suggests not to sign anything. Pause, reflect, and seek wisdom. If you're three or seven figures richer, do not go on a spending spree. Will a new Dodge Charger or a pair of upscale sunglasses be a game changer in two years? Think past your wants to what is needed to be successful in the long run. Develop second, third, and fourth-generational thinking. Always keep in mind that blessings are far more than "stuff."

For a list of my favorite books on understanding and developing your plan and legacy, please see the appendix. Feel free to send me your suggested reading on wheat pennies.

CURSES

After one of their relative's funerals, my mother and her sister meandered in the loved one's house, around stacks of newspapers and *Life* magazines. Cars collected for restoration adorned the front yard. The dear relative left a legion of unspayed, indoor cats. The household overwhelmed. Both neat freaks, my mom and aunt itched to pull out the disinfectant tucked in their bags and launch a concerted spraying. The same question we ask of blessing pertains to curses. What to do with the things of another's life?

When a loved one passes, the baggage of a lifetime washes to the shore, like a shipwreck's debris. Wood barnacled for years, steel-rusted and salt-bit, *the stuff* surfaces and must be handled. Grief is waylaid by the cleaning-up and cleaning-out of keepsakes

that meant something to them, but to us, resembles work. A lifetime of pictures, fishing gear, broken jewelry, pots and pans awaits our sorting. Sometimes this amounts to throwing things in boxes and carting them to our houses, thereby adding to our own collections. Other times, we treat the mess as junk and haul it straight to the dump or a donation center. My family's particular mode has been to utilize storage units. After all, out of sight, out of mind. Whatever we decide about the objects, most of us get less than a week to emote before the business of death knocks.

Honestly, I would have let my parents' extensive Christmas décor hide in the closet of their house, but for one reason—a home not lived in deteriorates. Too, we needed to sell the property, whether my heart was ready for that or not. After my sister and I had spent all day boxing, I was done. I still had a three-hour drive home, but she was determined to tackle the upstairs closet. Then, a nostalgic mood overcame her.

Not so for me. I kicked the creepy, stuffed Santa. "Let's toss all this."

Instead, my sister plopped on the floor, pulled the lid off a box, and whispered my name. Love letters written by my parents to each other more than fifty years past had been stuffed in a shoebox. By slowing down, my sister had uncovered a jewel among *Readers' Digest* books and fake greenery. She had discovered something hidden beneath the curses.

Ponder Point When you are going through your loved ones' items, have a trusted family member or friend come alongside you to help. They have fresh eyes to see things in a different way. Otherwise, you might toss the most meaningful treasure left you.

Since material items must be packed up quickly, consider boxing and sorting at a later date. My parents' letters were in a shoebox, and I could have easily slipped them in a discard pile without the curiosity and blessing of my sister's company.

DIRTY LAUNDRY

My friend's father had died. Her mother, Bev, and she had mourned and comforted one another. Then, months in, her mom's tears had dried up, replaced by anger. Bev pecked the dinner table with her fingernail. "I can't believe he did that."

As it turned out, my friend's father had committed several adulteries. Before she could stop her mother, this daddy's girl was listening to a detailed listing of her father's indiscretions. Bev had started with the family's first neighborhood. My friend's earliest childhood memory of racing to her mother's closet for her birthday present, a live turtle in its own rock domain, was scarred by knowing her father and the neighbor woman next door had consummated their illicit act there.

More images were counted off by her mother, in graphic detail, with names of people the daughter knew. She was stunned. She had always believed in truth, but this wasn't what she needed to hear, or even knew if she should. In twelve-step programs, these are called inventories. They're heralded as great movements toward healing. They were never meant for a daughter or son to hear, however. But this daughter did not know what to do with her mother's pain or loneliness. So, she listened to all the dirty laundry.

In another situation, John preached his mother's funeral. "She was really a great woman," he said. Then, John confessed his mother's hidden habit of shopping. She had cost him. This son had to round up five figures of cash to get his dad through the month.

Most of us have some dirty laundry. We hide secrets, the ugly gifts our loved ones might very well unwrap. These two adult children were not only dealing with loss, but with the aftermath of their parents' mistakes, the repercussions of their downfalls.

Of course, no parent, or person lives a spotless life. Most inheritances include both good and bad memories. Stories like these serve as reminders our loved ones were far from perfect, even when truth seems to ruin a childhood memory. We as inheritors of family memories must use a wide lens to examine a family member's life. To narrow a life lived to one memory, good or bad, is an unbalanced way of seeing their lives.

The dark secrets of our loved ones are not the things of fairy tales. However, these hardships are often the stories most telling of lives lived and pain overcome.

Ponder Point Being bequeathed hardships is one of the more difficult journeys we must take. Truly, we all have needed to not only forgive, but be forgiven. How another handles dirty laundry is up to them. How you wash yours is on you. Work on forgiving. Eventually, Bev and her daughter, and John were able to forgive their loved ones.

My friends learned valuable lessons to beware of what we are slated to leave our next generation. I have only to dig up old journals with overly descriptive details or scraps of papers written with rants about people to confirm my need for a good spiritual and physical housecleaning. It would be remiss of me to leave them for my next generation. Blessedly, we have time yet to clean out our dirty laundry.

Take fifteen minutes a day on a timer and go through a journal, skimming to see if it's something you want your children to read. Throw it away, if not.

Check old photos, or have a friend sort them, discarding that which adds nothing. Examine digital documents and media. Even more, this is a great time to take an integrity check. If you have something currently in your files you would be ashamed your children found, remove it now. Perhaps it's time to disengage from that sort of activity all together.

An ancient proverb says:

"Let your eyes look directly forward,
And your gaze be straight before you.
Ponder the path of your feet;
Then all your ways will be sure.
Do not swerve to the right or to the left;
Turn your foot away from evil."

~ Proverbs 4:25-27 (ESV)

If Your Job Deals with Death Daily

Fall tinted the skies. The safety officer from the fire department fished the pond sitting on the south acreage of my farm. I plopped down beside him.

"How's the fishing, Dave?"

"It's not been good lately."

Seemed like many things had not been good with him lately. The pandemic of 2020 had challenged our first responders. He told me of the procedure his people had to go through to enter and exit a house.

"They look like Michelin men going in." The multi-layers of protections, then the process of thorough cleaning coming out, he described them all.

"See that white object across from the pond?"

I knew what he was talking about. My small barn's generator ran on propane. The tank had bothered me for two years. When they planted the camellias around it, my young landscaper forgot to plant one in front of it, where I'd originally wanted the greenery.

"If you stare at it long enough, it looks like a woman in a white dress." He paused to reel an empty line in. "Who's hung herself." Dave wrestled the line from a snag.

"You've been troubled the last two times we talked. What's up?"

"My birthday was Sunday. I'm old."

Dave turned seventy-four. He has seen enough death. He has tried to rescue enough people, including the owners of the land I own now. His wife had battled cancer. Dave was mad at death. Sick and tired.

For the fourth time this week, friends have told me how they hated this virus. We barely remember the early days when two weeks off would give the needed time for this to die down. A year and a half later, political views rage online. We are all still waiting for the "perfect" day to come.

I have good and bad news. From an online search, some viruses have been all but eradicated from the world, such as smallpox and polio. Others have been controlled in many parts of the world due to preventions.

Yet my nurse friend, who works pulmonary and now the COVID-19 ward, reminds me that the humble prairie dog, a critter in the Midwest, carries a form of the Bubonic plague.

Cases of transmission to humans is extremely small, but this notorious disease,

"The world is indeed full of peril, and in it there are many dark places; but still there is much that is fair, and though in all lands love is now mingled with grief, it grows perhaps the greater."

~ J.R.R. Tolkien

even to this day, carries the stigma of having decimated medieval Europe.

The present-day virus, although a worldwide and deeply personal tragedy for us all, does not come close to the death numbers of that century. We can thank the researchers for their earnest pursuits of which we benefit.

Even knowing this, death hounds us, particularly when we work the medical units or the first responses, when we direct funerals or lead memorials, when we stand in a group, wondering who might be contagious.

An ancient poet wrote this:

"For everything there is a season, and time for every matter under heaven:

A time to be born, and a time to die…

A time to weep, and a time to laugh,

A time to mourn, and a time to dance…

A time to keep, and a time to cast away…."

Seeing death, witnessing it as Dave has day in and out, weighs on him. Becoming a year older adds to the message, "Your day is coming."

A sky-lit pond. A propane tank resembling a hanging woman. We live in the juxtaposition.

Ponder Point My fishing pal comes to the pond to be alone, to think and pray. There's no easy fix for death. Dave finds a doable peace by casting his line, hoping to catch and release the elusive twenty-five-inch bass. He may hate birthdays, but he's grateful for another day to dance with his wife and to keep his department serving well.

We all are carrying feelings around about the hard year, be it the last one, or another. Finding gratitude for the good moments, small as they may be, cracks the darkness with hope-filled light.

WHEN A FAMILY MEMBER IGNORES THE WILL

A relative told me about a beautiful wooden boat his grandfather had gifted him in his will. Slick and shipshape, this handcrafted boat was his grandfather's pride and joy. Many hours they had spent cruising lake waters, buffing wood, and caring for the engine.

The grandson was touched to tears when gifted this by a man he respected and loved. Knowing wills have a process, the young man counted on the executor, another family member, to release this meaningful gift to him.

He waited and waited. Meanwhile, the boat set outside in the weather, turning from a polished brown to a dull gray. Grass swallowed the beauty. The birds called the cushions home. A black snake adopted the boat trailer's tire rim.

This relative not only watched the boat fall into disrepair, but had to ask, plead, and beg for the executor to act. Sadly, the family member did not, and as it turns out, years later, has still not relinquished the grandfather's boat to its intended.

Taking recourse is a tricky matter for those of us who do not like to stir the pot. Challenging and confronting the family member, who serves as executor, is disheartening. It is not worth the effort, many of us feel. To counterpoint, losing a gift particularly assigned to a named individual only adds to the emotions surrounding the loss of a loved one.

Facts come into play here. A will is a legal document. Legal documents have requirements that must be fulfilled, whether by an assigned lawyer, family member, or friend.

The wishes are a contract that must be upheld. If we are the aggrieved person being denied a gift, we need to recognize, hard or not, the executor must perform these duties.

Ponder Point If an executor is a family member or friend and is not executing the will, the best recourse is to seek legal counsel. If you're not yet ready to go to that length, consider the recourse given in the Bible.

Go to the family member or friend, after time spent preparing for the encounter, and speak in a considerate, yet concerned manner about the execution of the will. If no understanding comes, bring other family members or friends. Choose to be a peacemaker, yet be firm. Determine to speak in a team fashion, not a one-on-one wrestling match. Coercion does not help.

After this, seek a lawyer if the executor chooses not to fulfill the requirements of the will.

So much is learned in the paperwork of estates. After the flowers die, after you've had time to rest, consider who you choose as executor for your estate, big or small. A sloppy executor does not bless your loved ones and only curses them. And if you have been appointed as an executor, you must complete the will's assignments.

FORGETFULNESS

My debit card has been missing for four weeks. I'd have canceled the card by now, but for one certainty. It was last used in my house, by me, and stashed in some unremembered place.

Two days ago, I ordered grocery delivery with my credit card. Having learned my lesson, I shoved the card into my wallet, marking my move. Yet somehow, it is not there. I have searched. It's gone. Screaming at the heavens is an option, except I forgot to check the weather before hiking off my frustration. A thunderstorm hovers the farm, and lightning strikes tall objects like me. I'm rather certain a bolt of lightning is not protocol for restoring my memory.

Especially during loss, our minds reroute into many directions. Our conversations, if we talk, are scattered as acorns battering a steel roof. The common phrases of our days seem to be—"What was I saying?" "I don't remember *that*." "Where is my car parked?" "What day is it?" "Did I eat dinner last night?" We people the land of forgetting.

Upcoming dates—written down many times—are ignored. I want only to curl up outside as the storm rolls in. Let the rain cool the air between the stress of forgetting and me. Instead, I must rescue my book from rain ruin because I forgot to bring it in from the patio. In the distance, the young landscaper ignores the storm, staking my newly planted apple and pear trees.

Now I remember. I gave him my credit card to buy supplies.

For this moment, forgetfulness is solved. Other times, it takes hours and days, if then, to be reconciled.

Ponder Point Some of us, after a loved one's death, have space to wander through days. Some of us cannot. My mother passed late afternoon. By evening, I slumped in a folding chair at my daughter's mandatory cheer practice, complete with an eight-count measure and loud music.

An ancient text advises us to take care of this day's worries only, as these are enough.

Seek immediate resources. Friends or family members, who are organizationally gifted, can create day-by-day lists, in order of importance, for you to follow. Have them snapshot them, as losing them is a reality.

Identify a trusted family member to handle the necessary bills to be paid. After a loss, I handed my monthly expenses over to the next of kin, resulting in a garnishment of property taxes. Choose a proven loved one who will not land you in a harder place.

Most of all, walk this day. It is enough to handle.

HI, I USED TO BE AN EXTROVERT

We have told the story over and over, how the loved one passed, the weeks before, the day before, the minutes before, the after. Extroverts often process things by speaking. But suddenly, we stop. Our hearts fill full of something we cannot name or even understand at this point, but here we are—silent.

Summer quiet slips into a faint fall wind. We ponder going to shop or church or inviting our children to lunch outside in the yard. We wonder if the car's battery will still start. We could text people our words, our fullness, our unknown feeling. Yet the deepest part of us swells into a wave covering our souls. We could try to discover what this is. But it seems untouchable right this moment, unknowable as our next months of life.

If we are fortunate, we live in a private place where we can walk, be it a large city, a country field, or the Appalachian Trail. When we walk, we do not find peace, but we are doing something, if only a lap around a deserted track.

One friend started walking. The miles turned into three, into ten, into fifty for months on end. By herself, in rain, sleet, or mosquito heat. Her thoughts focused on the next step, a loose rock, a raised tree root, the wet leaves littering the trail.

A year after her mother passed, another friend told me she had holed up in bed, not able to move, holding a book on the same page, staring at the words for hours. She would get up and dress before her husband came home. This gregarious friend, who used to rule a room when she entered, struggled to do life as she once had. The shock was she did not tell me this. We talk about everything. But on this, she was silent.

We come to the end of words, even to those closest to us. We settle in silence because the soul's cry is inexplicable to relay. No, that's not it. We do not have the strength or desire to speak. The humidity of loss smothers us, and we know—we just know—we must wait for the weather of our hearts to lift. We cannot foresee relief. Yet, we have seen it in others. Hope is far across the mountain we hike.

Ponder Point By now, we are sick of people telling us to take care of ourselves. Yet we must, for the sake of our people. Remember water. Fight for sleep. Take a vitamin. Get sunshine. Open an inspirational book if only for one line. Walk.

From Barely There to Hyperaware

My friend showed me the scars from bee stings that sent her to the hospital. Another has battled years to get off dialysis. A tick, the size of a poppyseed, targeted my relative's back, while another had a nine-centimeter mass removed. Another family member fought a mental health issue that gripped her like chains.

Following the dog, I trudged through the pond's overgrowth, late summer's explosion of weeds reaching to the fence line. Newly planted bushes hid the barn's generator. The camellias did not hide the two copperheads stretching across my path.

We check under our beds and tables for crawling things. Bushes are trimmed low to allow a visual inside the greenery. We determine to take our supplements. If we're brave, we strap on the blood pressure cuff, hoping for a perfect number. We shake as we drive because one wrong lane change might have us smashing into a car we missed seeing. Is today our last?

The world we live in, the seen and the unseen, is one scary mess. This is without adding viruses or other international tragedies. Somewhere in this journey, fear has morphed from not just what might break into our houses, to that over which we have no control. Nature, biology, psychology, chemistry.

Last night, all these worries attached to me like steel powder to a magnet. I was coated in how to protect others and myself. It was one of the most honest days I've lived in almost five years. Life no longer held the mystery of adventure, but the unknown of a million deaths. Adrenaline zipped my veins. My throat clutched.

After a death, we become hyperaware of all that can go wrong. We wake to find our hands crossed over our bodies, our jaws clenched, our shoulders tense. We're grateful for six or seven hours of respite, but our sleep tells us another story. Our haunts have haunted us in the dreams edging our memories.

A crossroads presented itself. Why did these snakes in the field bother me more than the three I had found near the house? Why did all these thoughts of people hit at once?

What was I to do? Should I truly live in

Life is real!
Life is earnest!
And the grave is not its goal;
Dust thou art,
to dust returnest,
Was not spoken
of the soul.

~ Henry Wadsworth Longfellow

this world, filled with its dangers or hide away? Use the elliptical or ride the stationary instead of cycling a country road, filled with wooden fences and horses, pavement, and pain?

It stunned me. I had no choice. I had lived five decades, through all sorts of pain. People I loved lived and died. I either let snake skins stop me, or walk on by, sensibly of course, and work around the creepy crawlies, and breathe in the unseen invaders.

I had to decide to live truth or live a false narrative that I controlled the universe, and all the molecules within. We each come to this point. We are confronted every time the flowers die.

Ponder Point How are we going to live going forward? How do we find peace in peril? This has been the question of the ages. Many answers have been given. You're probably tired of them. Pray. Journal. Talk. All good things. The granddaddy of them all seems to be the word "trust." Honestly, you have to seek what brings you this.

As for me and my house, I have sought God. The ancient Psalmist, David, writes:

"The Lord will keep
your going out and your coming in
from this time forth and forevermore."

~ Psalm 121

PANGAEA OR CONTINENTS: WHICH WAY WILL THE SIBLINGS GO?

Pangaea Pangea / (pæn'dʒiːə)
Noun: the ancient supercontinent, comprising all the present continents joined together, which began to break up about 200 million years ago (Dictionary.com).

Their parents both passed within three years of one another. The last good conversation among the brothers and sisters was then. Documents, death certificates, the work of stuff became preeminent. If they gathered, it was to discuss non-relational matters with an occasional family update. It was clear the sibling relationship had spiraled into distance and disconnect.

A funny thing happened on the way to a necessary family meeting. One brother was convinced by his tweens to watch "Frozen 2." The man was transfixed. The words of Olaf, the cartoon philosopher of this age, challenged him.

In the movie, the talking snowman works out a problem, as we all should, with a song. "When you are older, absolutely everything makes sense," the winter sage of insight and fun, Olaf, sings.

This man wondered if the snowman's wisdom, layered in irony, could help the familial discord. The brother recognized the family was journeying through unknown experiences that did not make sense. Although many decades old, the siblings, including himself, were reacting in childlike ways at times. The once-sweet fragrance of siblinghood had devolved into a smoke-filled room. Situations were hidden or discounted. Legitimate questions went unanswered. The "other" side responded with personal attacks or counter questions.

When had his maturity melted? Until his feelings were acknowledged, he could not make sense of many situations or be a help in the discord. With this recognition came clarity. The brother chose not to fall into indifference with his siblings.

"Help." His one-word prayer gave him the gumption he needed.

At the meeting, the brother did the unexpected. He greeted all his siblings with a hug. Before the scholarly sibling could whip out a PowerPoint, this brother suggested the family share how they were doing. Lest his man-card be revoked, he mentioned the idea came from his wife and her small group of friends who check in with each other monthly.

Turns out, the siblings all held common ground. They'd all been grieving the back-to-back deaths of their parents. Deeper still, none of them felt like celebrating Christmas. Even more, being older meant being adults, the grownups in the room, who worked through issues.

As siblings know who have been left material items jointly, be they large or small, getting together and sorting through issues is necessary. What is not counted on are the conversations that start behind one another's back, often becoming an "us" vs. "them" mentality, or even worse, a bad viral video.

Before and after the flowers die, it is wise to keep in mind stuff never trumps relationships. What's important in the end is family.

Ponder Point The work of stuff still demands attention and answers. A shared past might be the impetus to start a new positive story of your family's history. If we step outside our normal patterns, life-giving ways and moments are possible to unite relationships gone adrift. Individual movements toward goodness might affect the whole. Continents can sometimes reunite.

WHEN THE SIBLING GOES CONTINENTAL

The immediate matters have settled. Yet the loss of a loved one has occurred in another way.

"He looks like he's over us," one sister lamented. "My brother could care less."

Death comes in many forms, but the loss of a family member's closeness after a physical one can level us. The end of a living relationship is a rejection, knowing a sibling and often, a childhood friend, has chosen to part ways. To be dismissed from another's life shifts our internal world even more seismically. Everything we counted on is upended. The united family has divided.

"Even our misfortunes are a part of our belongings."

~ Antoine de Saint-Exupery

The many good memories we've shared with a person who moves and lives in this world now have an end date. We wonder if they miss our relationship. We seek clues to the relationship going quiet. "How are you?" we ask. When we want to ask, "What happened?"

"Everything's fine," they say one last time.

No, it's not. Ignored messages, phone calls or letters, and blocked social media are all evidence this relationship is dead.

But we can't force a solution.

Perhaps on their side, they see a wrong we've committed we do not. Or they are ashamed or guilt-ridden. So much time has lapsed, they don't see how the continents can be united again.

The problem compounds. Often their immediate family follows the disconnect. Cousins and other relatives try to navigate around the distanced family. A difficult and lonely task given events such as holidays, weddings, and more flowers dying.

Breaking up is hard to do, especially when it was not the way we wish it. Relationships bring steadiness. Losing the person we've known longest is gut-wrenching.

Ponder Point During the funeral, family often bonds together and shares the common goal of getting through the planning, the service, the estate. You often feel closer than you've felt for years with your siblings. Then, the continental drift occurs. What was once considered a solid relationship is crushed. The whole has divided.

Trying to make sense of the unexpected distance adds to the loss. To aid in understanding, write a letter to your family member you don't send. Tuck it away and revisit months later. Then, using discernment, decide whether to mail or not.

"Why bother? It won't change anything." True, but getting the angst on paper or speaking it to the sky transfers the onus onto something, or if you're spiritual, someone else.

This is a journey of living grief. No "once and done" exists here. Keep your side of the street clean. Surrender the control you think you have over your sibling. You don't. What they do is up to them.

When I Heal, um, No

The wife of a famous sport's figure offered our portable church their property on Sundays. Since I was on the location search team, I visited the facility and had the privilege of meeting her in an outdoor shelter, complete with fireplace and picnic benches. As the team considered how services might work, the woman wandered to a rocking chair. The one beside her was empty, beckoning me.

But I have this problem. Famous people stymie me. I can't think around them.

"I've been asked that a million times," they'd say every time I met the rich and famous. It's always good to be reminded nothing original comes from one's mouth. Thus, I have a no-celebrity rule. Others may rush in, but I've learned the value of holding back.

Yet I hurt for her, this mother who'd lost her adult child. "May I join you?" I asked.

She nodded. We rocked. Silenced ensued.

I might not speak to newsworthy people, but I couldn't neglect the grieving. "How are you?"

She stared into the trees darkening her land. "I'm okay."

"I imagine your work with the foundation helps." Perky positive words leapt from my mouth quicker than I could slap my trap. So much for my rule.

The rocking slowed. "Why is that?"

"Probably helpful in the healing process." My voice lifted at the end, knowing the conversation had pivoted and it was my fault.

Her feet unhitched from the rocker's foot bar. The chair halted. "You know. I've heard that a million times." The evening hid the lines on her face I'd seen earlier in the sunset. "Losing a child is not something you *heal* from."

Blood flooded my chest, leaving my limbs emptied.

"My heart will heal around this hole. It will never be healed from this. From losing him."

How these words soaked into my memory. Since that evening, I've attended more grieving parents than I ever thought. The fourteen in car wrecks. The multiple heroin overdoses. The suicides.

I recall the summer in the fourteen-year old's eyes, the creative spirit in another who overdosed, the kindness in the other. One had straightened his running shoes outside the closet he hung himself in. Their smiles, their greetings, the shy way one answered my question in Sunday school—I remember them all.

The children who leave us are not their deaths. Their lives are weighted with too much glory and richness for that to overshadow.

Yet our hearts settle around the grief of losing the beauty and light. Yes, laughter and joy rejoin our worlds. But we do not get over the loss.

When we heal, um, no. Not this side of eternity.

Ponder Point We've heard the sayings a million times. Our loved ones are better off. Or now they're reunited with others who have gone before. An old song even declares, "Only the good die young."

Anger over well-intentioned, yet careless words diminishes after the initial wave of condolences. We become accustomed to the talk. We stare. We attempt cordiality. We become numb.

The word itself, "healing," is loaded, as is the phrase, "getting over loss." In the end, after taking a class on working through grief, I've learned to do the hard thing—be merciful with people and their words, as this woman who'd lost her adult son was to me. We don't have to linger in conversation with them, nor should we retaliate either.

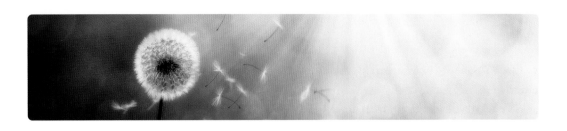

DECISION FATIGUE

After disposing of the medications, after the sheets were washed, after the last crusty casserole was dumped, after the dishes were cleaned, we found ourselves checking an empty house. Someone was missing.

For the first month or so, for one woman, it was a time to unlearn. The phone did not need to be answered. The mornings did not have to be scheduled between her sick mother and teens. A meal could be eaten without jumping up to help.

Yet after this first month, she was ready to have her mother back. Instead, decisions came. Who was selling the house? Who was taking Grandma's silver? What in the world happens to a decades-old mink coat?

On top of the questions, the work to cancel subscriptions, from paper and digital, to boxed meat and jam clubs added extra into this young mom's day, already given to raising kids, paying bills, and connecting with a husband. Further, the day came when the mailbox brought her loved one's death certificate. Necessary documentation for decisions, to be sure, but holding the physical paper drained the last drop of energy she had.

For me, something happened on the way to making decisions. I developed a habit. A nasty one. Snapping to make decisions became standard operating procedure. Looking back, I focused on getting problems solved quickly, rather than rightly.

The snap decisions were followed by worry of earthquake magnitude. Questions kept me up at night by imagining a hundred different scenarios in which my "yeses" might cause financial, mental, or emotional harm to my family. No matter what I decided, the answer haunted me. Of course, all this thinking only short-circuited what I really needed to be doing—grieving. But here I was.

Months down the road, albeit two years, when my life was hammered by a relational breakdown, I ended up in the counselor's office. Dead on my feet, I still had to make decisions about my parents' matters, and now about this relationship. Plus, another relative was mentally and physically walking a dangerous road.

"Stop. Just stop," I shouted to life.

About this time, our rescue dog, Hubble, started experiencing severe seizures and pain. Could he make it another month? Did I have to determine the best treatment plan for him as well?

For years, I had been the manager of the family's comings and goings. But were my problem-solving skills effective? How should I make the decisions I needed to make? Did people accomplish this without wrinkled skin and a fractured mind?

I, like the young mother, was swamped.

Ponder Point Fortunately, my counselor not only listened to my angst, but had a solution. She said to group my decisions for the day, on note pad or cell list. Then ask the question of each decision—does this need to be made today? If so, tackle it. If it does not, table it and schedule for another day.

Further, ask the decision a question—can and should this be solved by me? If so, do it. If not, hand the decision to another who can, be it lawyer, accountant, other family members, or God.

Either way, shift the decision into a mental outbox and close the door on the concern.

SHOPPING THERAPY: DEVELOPING AN ADDICTION

I tossed my credit card to my oldest daughter. "Buy your sisters dresses and shoes. Whatever we need to walk down the aisle." I'd already bought from my store, with expedited delivery to my parents' house. Just in time for the funeral.

My daughter corralled us into cars to be on time. She had pulled it off. My family looked respectable. At the church, after reading the last Psalm I'd read to my mother, I walked across the wooden floor, stepped down the stairs, without slipping or tripping, in my new shoes.

After we hide our clothes and must-have totes in the depths of our closets, some of us go numb about this time. Others of us ramp up. I'm a hybrid. I do a bit of both.

Shopping became an escape. I bought a years' worth of Kindle books, Christmas pillows and throws for every room, and exercise clothes, because now I'd have time to get into shape. A perfect skillet from the chic kitchen store came in because now I would cook.

The delivery people became my friends, leaving my driveway with blessings of healthy drinks, protein bars, and smiles. Meanwhile, in the basement, empty cardboard boxes Eiffel towered near the packages of paper towels and toilet paper.

My one-click addiction pushed away any serious thought, until a question came forth.

"How is this any different than your bondage to alcohol, those twenty-four years?"

Addiction comes in all shapes and sizes. It preys on us in our weak moments, seducing us away from the harsh realities of our lives.

Days add up to weeks up to months and before we know it, the drink, the food, the shopping, the sex has transformed from comforter into taskmaster. The bill has come due.

Paying attention to our activities, either going numb or ramping up, is difficult. But in the end, it will save us.

As my momma would say, regarding bad habits, "There will be hell to pay." We do not want to add havoc to the loss we're going through.

Ponder Point Cry, cry, and cry some more. Cuss at the moon, if you must, but beware the "little foxes" that scavenge around, stealing our lives.

Watch for these words:

- *I deserve this.*
- *I'll quit tomorrow.*
- *I'll give myself another week.*
- *I can't do this without _____.*
- *It's only one glass, one pill, one bag of chips, one shopping cart.*
- *Other people are doing this. Why shouldn't I?*

The hard question we need to ask is, "Why Should I Do This?"

Obey your doctor. If they prescribe a sleep aid or anxiety help, take as advised. If we find ourselves, doubling the dose, tell someone. Same with the maxed-out credit card, the rum hidden behind the avocado oil, or the website with porn or gambling.

Living the first months of grief rocks the emotions. It's hard to be grown-up when we want to spin out of control in sadness. But our legacy is watching. We are setting the example for someone, young or old, in our handling of loss.

MEETING A SIBLING AFTER THE PARENT DIES

In her late teens, Anna was ready to meet the dad she had never seen. After walking away from his young daughter before her birth, this absentee father had continued down a harmful road involving substance abuse and illegal activities. Finally, after most of Anna's childhood and teen years had passed, this man had come clean and was considered stable. A meeting between Anna and her father had been scheduled. She could barely wait.

"She needs closure," Anna's mother thought, convinced her daughter would gain the necessary identity she needed to move forward.

"Love is a fire that will burn through every difficulty."
~ Andrew Murray

"I'm going to meet my dad," Anna said.

Then startling news came. Her father had overdosed. His body lingered, but brain waves were undetected. After prayers for a miracle were launched, the answer became clear. The medical devices were disconnected. He was gone.

Instead of meeting at a pancake house as planned, Anna saw her father's face in person for the first time as he lay in a casket. She had been afraid to go up front in the funeral home to visit him alone, but she had wanted to, and she did. After long minutes, Anna was surprised to be surrounded by half-a-dozen siblings, from several moms, whom her mother and she had never met. It was a family reunion unlike any other.

Anna connected deeply to one sister, as did their two mothers. Although raised apart and unknown to each other, the sisters had much in common, from their love of Asian food to their artistic natures and faith. Conversations led to the planning of a vacation with the two sisters.

A friendship was forged between the two mothers. Their daughters had struggled with the same issues. This relationship became a safe place for the moms to share and seek advice on raising their girls. They shared their lives as single mothers, who eventually married good men.

Although Anna never got to meet her father, her heart became rich in family by connecting with her sister. She has since become closer to another. Anna and her mother show how seeking others in friendship, amid the loss, can lead to an abundant life. They chose love over losing.

Ponder Point It is odd to miss what you never knew. Anna lives with questions only her father could have answered, but has chosen to remain focused in the present, instead of what could have been. Truly, we all come to a point where we must choose how we are going to move forward in our grief journeys.

In this age, the days of a two-parent household are an anomaly. Familial connections are up to the parents' discretion. However, the time comes when your child will make their own decisions as adults. Encourage them to seek wise counsel and steady consideration. Be the wisdom they seek.

Your attitude as parent and grandparent sets the tone. Take the high road.

THE WHAT IFS

His feet, soles up, came into view first, as his sister climbed the stairs. Please help, she prayed, for what she was about to see. The seconds ate at her.

"Don?" No answer. Was he dead?

A deep breath sickening her, she entered his room. His body lay in a straight line. "Don?" The position of his body bothered her. He had been a ball player before his disease robbed him of normalcy. He would never stay down without a fight. There had been none.

"Don!" She was afraid to touch him, yet she wanted him off his face. Emergency Services said not to move him. They had been to his house twice now, and EMT knew his frailty.

She covered his body with a blanket, tucking the edge in. "What happened?"

The EMT rushed up the stairs. "Mr. Bailey?"

"I found him." After waving them in the room, she moved away from his body. "His feet. I saw them from the stairs." Tears filled the gap. "He fell, it seems."

So did the fail safes this Friday the family had put into place for him. Adamantly opposed to an alert necklace, Don promised to carry his cell wherever he went. The device was found in his living room. Even so, the audio, set to automatically activate after two rings, shifted to voicemail. The woman who cleaned his house had changed her time to Monday. His daughter who stopped by on this day had an out-of-town visitor. Don's family group message contained nothing to be concerned by.

Yet something had gone wrong. The EMT rolled Don over. His sister backpedaled from the room. Decay had long started its course. Twenty-four hours had gone by, the family figured out later.

His son asked, "What if I'd not had the barbecue and gone to see Dad?"

"What if I hadn't moved my clean date?" the housecleaner asked.

The youngest daughter wondered, "What if I'd pushed for the medical alert?"

"What if I'd insisted on the night-time care?" the friend asked.

What if questions abound, but no answers come, nor can they. For every situation, a million different paths exist.

Ponder Point Stopping the flow of "What ifs" is not an instantaneous effort. Writing out the timeline of the situation, from the viewpoint of family members, might help give clarity and wisdom.

Acceptance wars with the "What ifs." The question is pernicious. Even if you think you've won the battle, you may find yourself haunted by it again. Give the "What if" a moment, then hand the question over in prayer, by journaling or to a friend.

LOSING A CHILD IN A TRAGIC MANNER

In the late 70s and 80s, malls had become the new downtown. This young woman had worked in both a Flowerama and a Hickory Farms. As a college woman fresh out on her own, she visited the one near her school to pick up perfume.

As she left the mall, a man with a beard handed her a card. "You'd be great as a model," he said.

She glanced at his face. "I'm late for class." She waved goodbye, knowing her grade would drop a number if she were late again.

"Seriously. Think about it."

She did. In this world of instant social media fame, it is hard to imagine how difficult being "discovered" used to be.

"I'm going to call this man." The young woman flashed the card to her closest friend. "This might be my big chance." She never quite understood why her friend hung out with the likes of her. Partying and guys, with studies on the side, was her motto. But her friend stayed.

"Something isn't right about this."

"He's a photographer. What couldn't be right?"

Her friend put her foot down. This was a bad idea. The young woman threw the card away, respecting her friend's wisdom.

Many months went by. One morning, the young woman picked up the Sunday edition. A hunt was underway for a missing twenty-year old. A photograph, a professional one, accompanied the article. Model-tall, the woman had styled her hair big and wore her shorts short.

A year later, this young woman was found. The person who took her life was a photographer. He solicited young women at the mall, the paper said. This young woman had allowed him to take hundreds of photographs of her. His actions seemed normal at first, then had slipped into something more insidious.

Her family, led by first-generation Cuban parents, became concerned about their daughter's close tie to this man. Having escaped their homeland's regime, they sought a better life for their adored daughter. Never did they expect her life to be ravaged. Never did they expect this horror.

Words are useless to those of us whose children are gone. Words are battering rams to those who have lost their children in a tragic manner.

More than that, our minds rewind over and over. We create scenarios. Sometimes we have been called to the scene. Memories imprint in our minds. We have seen too much. We have imagined too much. We have heard too much.

Life is too much. But we keep living. Others need us. That is all we have.

Ponder Point There are no words.

Staying Clean: Sobriety

The boutique hotel was themed with mirrored furniture and upscale furnishings. Most importantly, the restaurant served beef and Brussels sprouts. Outside the window beside my table, runners darted by, and friends, dining outside, laughed. All I wanted was to go upstairs, shower, and sleep.

Dinner lingered, not from my design. I took dessert with me, because, by golly, I deserved some sweet. After dinner, the elevator, wrapped graphically with a couple dancing the tango, whisked me to my floor. I carted my bags to the room, dropping them near the door. I checked the bathroom, thanking God for a tub and a large shower head.

I plonked my purse on the desk beside a five-dollar bottle of water and clicked on the TV to distract. The channel of happily-ever-afters popped up. If only for two hours, I needed to live in the predictable. During a commercial, I scanned the rest of the room. With its own price tag, the wine bottle waited for a taker on a side table.

Since 2001, I've been sober. My thoughts of drinking again have been nearly non-existent. If I did think it, whiffs of the aftermath swatted away the temptation. This night was different.

Alone in a hotel, after the roughest time of my life, after trying to protect my adult children, while recognizing their need to journey through pain, I wanted relief. The hip place did not satisfy. The dessert had not. The Happily-Ever-After channel was not bringing it. The soaking tub promised, but that would take too much work.

In seconds, the bottle grew in my mind to a six-foot tall seduction.

"I'll take the edge off," the wine suggested. "I'm just the thing, after what you've been through."

Naturally, it had to be red wine, my favorite years ago. I hoped it was a Cabernet. A Merlot might have melted me on the spot.

I could drink just one glass. Throw the rest of the bottle away.

Weakened, I gathered my emotional weapons. I ran through the scenario. A buzz was a way out, a short-term escape. The chance of stopping at one glass would never happen. A sulfite and sugar hangover, after drinking the whole bottle, was likely.

Then, I counted the real costs. Did I want to chain myself to the bottle again after twenty years? Had I not had the best years of my life, hard as they were, without alcohol to help me through? Had a drink ever done one thing for me, except leave me isolated and lonely?

The bottle shrank. I grabbed the water instead and slept the sleep of angels singing over me.

Ponder Point Be it one day or many years, don't forget the deep diving work our souls did and still do to overcome our addiction. Our grasp at temporary comfort, our fixes, are finite. Remember the long game of sobriety. No matter the circumstances. After the flowers die, you need to be present.

Temptations will arise. Your haunts might track you down, be they gambling, casual sex, smoking, and the like. Although you are weak and tired, now is not the time to indulge. Call a friend. Tell them exactly what is tempting you. Remember the relationships at stake. Remember your well-being that would be destroyed.

Walk through the past you've lived, the uselessness of your addiction. Attend a meeting. Remove the bottle, the TV, the cell phone, whatever it takes to slay the enemy that only seeks to destroy your life. One. Day. At. A. Time.

THE WALL

Vacation time or personal days are not options. Projects, under our watch, are due. By this time, we are sick of telling *the story*, messaging the story, or watching people avoid asking about the story.

Yet, we must interact with people. The multiple hats we all wear require action and face-to-face communication.

"I'll make the deadline," we speak morning and night.

We map out the way, knowing how many hours are needed to make the project timely.

But we hit The Wall.

We do not want to show up for work. We do not want to open our calendars. We do not want to read messages tagged "Urgent." We do not want to think of dinner.

The only thing we want to do, besides sleep, is tie a brick to our planners, and hoist the scribbled squares into a deep lake. One we hope houses a Loch Ness Monster that devours such things.

But we are the adults. We have to do those things.

However, things have a way of stonewalling.

For me, the most beautiful cat in the world, the family feline, Luna, lives up to her translation. She waxes and wanes like the moon. Everyone should have a high-maintenance cat once in their lives, if they are seeking to grow character and are committed to learning about long-term difficult relationships.

Angry at whatever felines are angered by, Luna started "marking" her territory on my favorite couch. Never had she done this before.

The scent permeated the air, mimicking the hospital my family had held vigil in. Disturbed by the loss in our house, or the lack of treats caused by our absence, Luna, to be colloquial and literal, was PO'd.

Oddly, the run-in with the cat was it. The wall towered over me, too long to go around, with one way out. Over. I tied a metaphorical hook to a metaphorical rope, and cast the weight into the air, trying to reach over the wall. Frustration, cries of help, words I hadn't used in years, anger, all occupied my attempts.

"Now may the Lord of peace himself give you peace at all times in every way."

~ 2 Thessalonians 3:16 (ESV)

At last, one tug told me the rope held. All I had to do was climb, with ligaments and tendons aching, and knees scraping rock.

But I clung, with fingers jammed into handholds and forearms trembling. This, my friends, is what we do. We cling and push and pull ourselves up, with help from those surrounding us, and if we believe, God. We follow the pattern Winston Churchill gave the Allies at the pivotal moment in World War II. We never give up. We never give up. We never give up.

Ponder Point Hang on. That's all I got. Hang on. Stay with it. Take a deep breath. Hang on.

THE EX-SPOUSE, AKA, THE DISENFRANCHISED MEMBER

They were a blended family of forty years. Not a smooth blend, like grandma's mashed potatoes with nary a lump in the pot. More like the beef soup some dads make before football games, a conglomeration resounding for days, for better or worse, depending on available ingredients.

The children, both teens and young adults, converged in celebration, for game nights and in emergencies. They never aired their disagreements in public. Going deeper to create unity, the family had strategized during a long, but winsome Saturday, on their family's core values. Integrity, honesty, humor, connection, and generosity were decided upon as the guideposts for their actions.

Enter stage right the person who is a family member to some—the ex-spouse, the father. Communication with him had always been encouraged for the good of the children. Going social about family details was not.

Then, tragedy struck. After an extensive hospitalization, the mother passed away, the parent who was the common denominator of all the children.

Her ex-spouse, father to three of them, ran amuck. Often involved in scenarios causing havoc in their adult children's lives, he decided to dole out personal details about their mother's passing on media sites. Every member of the family was irked by the socialization of the tragedy. The father was asked to remove the information.

"It's how I handle grief," the man said. "Besides that, it's good for her old friends to know." Despite the request he posted again to a social media site.

Many people mean well. But some enjoy the attention of breaking bad news. This man saw a crisis and thrived on the turn of dramatic events. It is a travesty to see adult children out-adult their parents, but selfish behavior oft outweighs balance. We cannot control others.

Ponder Point If you have social media, hide or block people's posts that trigger a response. If you are staying away from social media and are approached with a story by a friend, consider stopping that person from sharing the dirty laundry.

We live in the day when multiple devices route our most private moments to multiple sites. Hard as it is, avoid revenge and take the high road. Maintain your composure, thereby setting the tone of interaction. If you find it still bothers you months later, and it very well might, make an inventory of all the bothersome actions the person has committed. Burn your list so none of your children find it, after you're gone.

People can bother us only as long as we allow them.

The Worse Brings
Out the Worst:
The Narcissist

My friend had lost her mother the previous week.

"He's gone," she said.

"Who?" I asked.

She twisted her hair into a clip. With or without makeup, this woman represented beauty to her DNA. "John."

"A business trip?" I asked, knowing her husband traveled like most of us frequent the bathroom.

"No. Gone. Gone. He left me." She paused as I grabbed her hand. "After everybody left the house. I slept in my dress. I couldn't unzip it."

A day before the funeral, she had asked him to fix a kitchen cabinet. People would be at the house, bringing food. She did not want the cabinet door hanging by a hinge, exposing their toaster and other appliances. He blew up at her, telling her how hard this road had been for him, how she had neglected and hurt him.

"He'd already packed." Her husband had deemed his presence necessary during the funeral and during the house reception afterwards. He had been generous, he had told her, in lasting that long.

A person's true colors often come out after the funeral. The stickers stick. The fair-weather folk flee.

Those who only think about themself and their happiness seem to lack, or truly do lack, the ability to empathize with your pain. Stunningly, these people are often those we have known in intimate ways, be it spouse or relative or friend.

Another friend's daughter arranged a family gathering weeks after her grandmother's passing. The father was touched by the generosity of his daughter's spirit.

The wife pulled her husband aside, as the adult children brought in food. "I'm left out of everything. You didn't tell me about this."

He was stunned. Their daughter had included everyone in the family invitation, including her mother. "You saw the text. She called us both."

"It's all about you. How you feel. How worried everyone is about you."

This grieving man pointed out the family was gathering to share this moment in time, to connect with everyone, to laugh, to remember, to talk about something other than death. The mother pouted through the meal, responding with curt answers.

"What's up with Mom?" The daughter asked the father.

Mom was up with Mom. This is not a clinical assessment. We'll leave that to the professionals. However, in the worst of times, of all the ugliness expressed by the loved ones left behind, this trait of narcissism seems the most egregious.

Being 'narcissistic' is described in the etymological dictionary as being "marked with excessive self-love."

It is unfortunate when we need comforting that another inserts malcontent into the family's story of grief.

Ponder Point Acknowledge the hurt this person is causing you. Turn to safe people. Recognize that no words will change this person. Your advice most likely would not be welcomed. Only this person can change this person.

Not Remembering the Memory Years Later

While I taught my fourth-grade Sunday school class, a man entered the room, alerting to a stranger's presence in the foyer.

"Someone's here to see Linda."

I motioned for her, my new co-teacher, to keep teaching, figuring the "someone" was a church member needing help in another class.

In the church foyer, Linda's estranged husband waited. "I need Linda."

I knew him. He would not come to church, and she did not want to see him.

"It's an emergency." His eyes were red, and his balance unstable. This man was either drunk or fighting a hard hangover.

I did not believe him.

Then, he uttered a word that floored me. "Please."

This man was not known for his polite behavior, or concern for others. Was he that desperate for another drink or fix? Something struck me, but I could not figure out what.

"Stay here." On the way back to class, I grabbed another to help with the kids' crafts.

"Fred's here," I whispered. Her arms crossed. Linda was not having any of his antics today.

"This sounds different." The word "emergency" stalled on my lips. "Something's different, Linda."

In the church's foyer, he said to Linda, "Your son is dead."

We both stared at him, wondering what disgusting game he was playing. Had he increased his drug usage? He was spiraling. Disbelief washed over both of us.

"What are you talking about, Fred? He's home. I drove by on the way to church."

"Did you see him?"

"His car was there." We studied Fred's eyes as if we could draw out the drugs from his body.

"His bathroom, Linda." Fred shook his head. "Shot himself."

"No. But his car."

"I found him. He's dead."

Linda dropped to the floor. I followed. I do not need to tell you anymore details. We've all lived them in some way.

That day brought many unforgettable memories. But a new realization came forth. Some of us remember with photographic quality the events we experience as our lives unwind.

Others of us completely forget the moment, for days, months, even years. This was Linda's experience.

Two years later, Linda and I talked about that morning. She had no recollection of me being with her, or the events that followed. She does not remember us poured out on the terrazzo floor, sobbing, my arms useless to hold her.

She does not remember her mind searching for an alternative place her son could be. "He's out back walking. That's where he is," Linda kept repeating. Or being told her son's body had been found.

She does not remember plying me with questions, begging for truth. I hated my words. "He's gone, Linda." Her cries to this day echo in my memory.

Ponder Point We each handle the hearing of a loved one's passing differently. Some we might remember. Others we tuck away.

Our minds, bodies and spirits are doing what they need to labor through this time. If you don't remember, and people are rushing to fill in the blanks, it can be overwhelming. Most are trying to help, yet they bungle. Ask them to wait until you're prepared to know.

PARENTING THE DIASPORA

A son had uncovered unsavory information. Dad had done wrong. Another son had not seen him in months. With limited conversation, a daughter had helped him settle into a new house. The older ones were hurt. Three were not speaking to one other. The youngest went to live with him.

Then, the father had an accident. Desperation and fear struck. Some of the children stayed at the ICU with him. Others did not. Emotions skyrocketed. Worry was constant about how their dad was reacting in the ICU, about how each of them were helping.

Their family had weathered decades of life together. Yet the mother had never seen her children more at odds. They always rallied together, but how long would they make it past the flowers dying?

Most of us have marveled at how six people can be in a room and see different aspects of an unfolding situation. We are mottled by our experiences, histories, and viewpoints, sometimes, even, sheer fatigue. To say we hold different perspectives is an understatement.

As family members, employees, and citizens, we have lived through unsettled and unknown times. We have disagreed with the way incidents were handled. We have known better. We were hurt, and possibly, wronged.

These days, the intent of all actions is assumed to be worse-case scenarios.

The other person meant evil. The other person could have stopped it. The other person was malicious. The other person deserved a tongue-lashing, if not downright excommunication or cancellation.

We have landed in a reality show and have the audacity to think we can direct the scenes, even when we can barely get out of bed, our hearts laden over our children's distance. Will it be possible, we fret, to be in the same room together again? For something more than a funeral?

Hang tight. The same qualities in our families that held us together through many storms are still there. Trust their character; trust yours.

Ponder Point An ancient proverb says, "Good sense makes one slow to anger, and it is his glory to overlook an offense."

Give yourself and your loved ones a timeout. Not the punishing kind. The processing one. The wound is fresh. Don't pick at it. Give space for your children to breathe and work their way through this. Respond and send texts with words carefully chosen, those of love and wisdom, when asked.

Stay committed to your family but respect their grief process.

DEAR GOD, I AM SAD

As I sit on the patio, before the sunrise, birds chirp, and a crescent moon shines over the maple. The peacocks call. The rooster crows. The woodpecker is thankfully non-peckish. All is goodness and light, yet I am sad.

Having risen early to seek God, I have not thought of Him once. Instead, letters to elected officials become more important to send. I am sad I've lost out on spiritual time that could refresh my soul.

I am sad when my cat crouches down, as if to mark the rug, and I swat her with my foot.

I am sad I spoke to my young adult last night in a harsh tone about being picky over leftovers.

"Depth of earnestness are stirred by depths of tribulation. Diamonds spark most amid the darkness."

~ Charles H. Spurgeon

I am sad I did not advocate for my loved ones more when they were in the hospital. I did not drive to see them enough, or pay attention to their faces while they slept, studying every detail. I am sad; I'm mad. Where did the friends of my loved ones go? Where were they in the days leading up to their passing?

I am sad my last words to my loved ones were inconsequential. As they lay mumbling, I pretended to know what they were saying, without trying to understand. I responded with trivia. I wasted their last breaths, and my final goodbyes.

I am sad my heart carries this weight, and all I can do is walk through this.

I am sad spring flowers have passed. Despite the heat, summer flowers fight to bloom, and their blossoms are ignored.

I am sad paperwork rules my life, from car registration renewals, to checks written, to holidays and birthdays celebrated.

I am sad the young men who work the farm do not know how to weed. I am sad that they do not understand pulling weeds by hand is necessary to get the root.

I am sad despite loss, life goes on. My daughter drives with the instructor. My sister has major surgery. I have not prayed for my friend in Colombia. I kneel at my empty bed at night and no words come forth.

I am sad sometimes the only word I utter is "help."

I am sad I ignore You, God.

Ponder Point Making myself feel better, I plea-bargain with my cat, who accepts the treat. A wash of pink surrounds the patio. I look up.

The sun has arced over the tree line. It has risen again, as it has since time began.

For a moment, all that matters is light, trees, and a doe. The unlikely happened—I looked up and did not miss this. But I miss them.

It is good to acknowledge the depths of the heart. Nobody can fix this. It's just a sad day.

TRIGGERS

Kaye crossed off each day until the CPR training for her job.

"I don't want to do this," she prayed. "You know I don't."

The five-day countdown came for the certification. "Can I get a break here?"

Eking out enough money to make bills, Kaye had made it a year alone. She needed this job. She needed to pass. If she could have heard one holy word from heaven, she said, it would have helped. But no words came. "I just don't get it."

The morning she dreaded came. Kaye arrived at the exact time, the last person to come. Groups circled their practice

"…in the sleepless night, the difficulties in connection with our family, our trade, our profession. Whatever tries us in any way, speak to the Lord about it."

~ L.B. Cowman

dummies. Focused, she stayed with the training, through the many hours necessary to learn again how to save a life.

After the final, she noticed something. Only she had checked off all the correct CPR actions, as indicated by a light on the testing model.

At her small group several days later, Kaye relayed how much she'd feared that day. Tears lit her eyes. "At least I know now I did everything to save him."

Employing her CPR training, Kaye had labored over him, but with results that did not end the way she wanted. Her man, her best friend, was gone. For one whole year, she had doubted herself, reliving what she might have done wrong.

Finally, she learned the truth of the matter. She had followed protocol to the letter. The CPR test confirmed her skill.

"Did it help, you passing the test perfectly?" Kaye was asked.

"Yes. I felt"—she paused searching for words—"like I moved forward."

Ponder Point Many of us relive aspects of the loss of our loved ones, whether driving a car for the first time after an accident, scrambling too many eggs in the morning, or carrying the mental image of the ventilator left in our loved one's mouth.

Harder still, getting confirmation you did all you could, or made the right decision often takes time. There's no easy way around this.

Given that, some of us are stuck. Some of us have waited. Some of us are on the edge of losing hope. Then a breakthrough occurs. At last, peace like air comes.

Ninja Skills Needed

The security alarm, a trusted friend when our loved ones were with us, turns on us one night. The alert shrills throughout the house. The dog, who barks at squirrels, goes apoplectic. The cats claw for cover. The teenagers come down the stairs, scratching their sleepy heads, wondering what is going on, instead of sheltering in the closet as instructed.

Our loved one handled the security of the house. The homestead was protected because this person knew what to do. Us? We grab our dad's old walking canes, kept in remembrance, and fling those and a B-rated cuss word, not even the bomb for heaven sakes, down the stairs.

Bravo, we've terrified the dog into counseling and drained any hope of sleep for the whole family.

However, the security scare, which happened to be a teen opening the door to take a picture of the moon for astronomy class, has revealed many valuable lessons.

We are as prepared for an intruder as we are a swarm of locust. Our first line of defense hinges on a keypad. Our second line of defense depends on the police getting to our house in time. The much-loved doors and windows of our home by day are our enemies at night. The dog is a liability, needing protecting.

It is an exceptional burden to present home security to a grieving one, but necessary. Names have been posted on the internet. Locations are known. Details are listed. We can ignore or be proactive.

Among all our connections—churches and synagogues, business associates, friends, adult children—someone knows about security and who to contact. Fortressing our homes takes one less problem off our worried minds.

Ponder Point An alarm is good. But a trusted and vetted security person will bolster your home with gear to strengthen, such as door jambs and driveway alarms. Outdoor lighting is key.

They will ask you questions, if you have a gun and are legally and properly trained to operate it. Other forms of protective gear are available, they will point out.

My friend, a popular podcast hunter, told me a trained dog is a great first line of defense. However, do not get the first stealthy pup who catches your eye. You must first determine if you are committed to caring and maintaining a dog. Do you travel often? What plans do you have to care for your animal? Does your lifestyle support caring for another living being? If so, have the security associate help choose the best dog, not puppy, for you.

If you decide to get a watch dog or a protection dog, realize they need continued training to keep their skills sharp. They are an investment. Dogs are a two-fold win, even the one that skitters away. They provide needed companionship in the dark of night.

Consider your second and third line of defense. Run scenarios with your family so that they rush away from danger and into a safe space. Practice pumps up your family's muscle memory to kick in.

It's too much, you say. I get this. But preparation whips worry. One small step each day helps. Remember your ultimate line of defense, prayer.

THE KINDNESS OF STRANGERS

The car smelled of old coffee, a melted protein bar, a half-eaten hamburger. The clothing bag given to me at the hospital had cooked in the North Carolina heat.

A car wash was imperative, a symbolic attempt to wash off germs and that smell. Splashes of lavender, blues, reds, and greens flashed through the windshield.

Panic arose. Just a minute or so, I shrieked at my claustrophobia as my car and I rolled through the drive-through wash. The tight space reminded me of the slim hospital room my loved one had been moved to after ICU.

After surviving the wash, I pulled over to the vacuum area. The young man in the next bay turned to me. A circular cord followed him.

"You want this?" He gestured with the tool in his hand.

I shouted. "I don't know what that is."

"Hold out your hand."

I sized him up. Kindness washed over his face. I held out my hand.

He blew a puff of air onto my skin. "It helps in small places. Like the cracks between seats."

I nodded my head. "I'm not worried about those."

"It helps my allergies," he said.

"You must be having a time of it." North Carolina is legend for its spring and summer yellow dusting. All that dastardly pollen helps makes us renowned for our honey-bees. Or so, we beekeepers brag.

"Yep. But Jehovah-Rapha has me."

I tried to remember what the meaning of that name was for God in the Old Testament.

"The Lord Who Heals," he said.

I nodded. "I'll pray for you today." Sidling to the other side of the car, I spoke a quick prayer. I was tired of supplication, mindfulness, good thoughts. Whatever the flavor, I was done. I'd wrestled the morning with God, pouring out angst, problems, and concerns. I even considered that my time on this earth might be over this very day since I saw little provision and no hope. Not giving up fully, I flung a hail-Mary prayer for preservation at Him, asking to be restored somehow. A miracle of sorts.

As the young man worked on his car beside mine, the one inherited from my dad, his words penetrated my hardened heart. I recalled the early morning sun

"One evening when we had a large campfire, my grandmother told me the story of how I got my name. She said that my name symbolized the rarest flower in all Cambodia, Vietnam, and Thailand. You could search through the whole forest and find only one."

~ Siv Ashley

shadowed in fog. An unexpected warm temperature had allowed me to sit outside. The geese had flown over the house. The sky had cleared to shine on the trees.

And lo and behold, if a sweet wave of refreshing did not pour over me as I wiped down the dashboard, as I swiped away the memories from the car spent weeks in a hospital parking garage. Precious light and life had been gifted to me this morning, and now, with the kind presence of this young man.

I prayed again for him, while he vacuumed every crevice in his car. I asked for healing, meaning the prayer more than the dictation of the one earlier. I exited my internal world and entered into someone else's. As I drove away, the young man waved me over. I lowered my window.

He took my hands. "God wants you to

know something." He gazed deeply. "He's glad you didn't give up." He squeezed a piece of paper in my hand. We smiled our goodbye.

I pulled the paper out of my purse at home. He had written his name down, drawing a crown beside it, which in our faith signifies indescribable goodness.

Thank you, my forever friend, Prynce.

Ponder Point Say a prayer. You have thought of so many people. Say one for yourself. Then open yourself to the mysteries that unfold and come your way.

HIS LIFE WAS TAKING OFF,
MY SON'S

On a mild fall night, Luke and his wife Gerri and I feasted over a crab boil prepared by my new favorite restaurant. We had often talked of going out to eat, but then their son had died four years earlier. The time never seemed right, until now.

This couple had helped thousands of others traverse the world of caskets or urns, opened or closed, music and memories, throughout their years as funeral directors. They never, as all parents do, wanted to be a client.

"I never expected to be here. On this side." Gerri tilted her head back, toward the night sky. "His life was taking off."

"It all stops. It comes to an end," her husband, Luke, added. "Life is never the same."

This couple knew grief and anguish over losing parents, but after the death of their son, the passage of time became the focus. Everything on the calendar was centered around that day, before that day, after that day.

At dinner, they showed me the pictures of the dogs their son had left behind, dressed in the crazy clothes he had bought them. His memory lingered in the air like the Marlboros Gerri smoked.

"It never leaves me. He never leaves me." A glimmer shined in Gerri's eye, hinting at the tears she had cried for almost fifteen hundred days. The kind that finds a moment's laughter, then fades into grief, into acceptance, into a scar.

"We're able to help like we haven't ever." Gerri smiled, the one loaded with more than happiness. "We're able to connect with families who are grieving their kids." This couple had arranged for premature babies and children to be picked up, while loving on the parents with a wisdom gained in the terrible doing.

They had gotten past the what ifs, the why, the rants, and grown into a couple that gives back, although it hurt every time. In this private moment, among the crickets' rhythm, a dog's howl, a turtle's splash, a sacred sadness surfaced. Our hearts deepened with the words, as much as the silence.

"I watch you. I watch all those who've lost children," I said. "It's the one club I never want to be a part of."

Luke nodded. "That's a good way to put it.

A club. You don't know. You just don't know until it comes to your door." The knowledge of the irrevocable seemed to hold them. "I didn't expect my life to go this way," he added.

"It's all different, each one we lose," Gerri said. "We see their value and worth so deeply after they're gone."

Somewhere in this grief walk, we live through enough funerals to realize we cannot prepare. Each varies, as each is unpredictable. Our minds search for a commonality, a way to classify or categorize grief into a room in our heart. Yet grief demands its separate way, its individual memories.

"It's been four years," Gerri said. Yesterday, it felt like the first Christmas, the first birthday, the first vacation. Yet today, "It's the anniversary."

Ponder Point Death has changed life. Others will expect normalcy after time. Your normal will never be the same. Others might not understand this.

IF YOUR SIGNIFICANT OTHER SHOWS NO EMOTION

Bringing a smile and joyous words, Sallie comes to my house every other Thursday. She does something for me that is better than a pedicure. She makes my house shiny and tidy.

Several years ago, after a loss in my life, Sallie shared hers. She had lost both her sons, one to a drug overdose and another to an accident.

"How are you even standing?"

She paused. "I'm not like this all the time."

If there ever were a Southern Mary Poppins in her middle age, Sallie would be it. Yet even the Poppins we know have their edgier days. Imagine how much more, given losses.

Recently, an event in my family revealed the different responses to grief. Sallie understood. "I asked my husband one time why he never showed any emotion. Why he never grieved over the passing of our boys." She brushed a curl that strayed from her ponytail, reminding me we had been young mothers once. "He loved them, no doubt."

"Did he answer you?" I asked.

"This is what he said. 'I don't grieve in front of you because if you're having a good moment, I don't want to bring you down.'"

He had also admitted, "Do you know how many moments I pull the truck over on the way to work, and I scream and cry? I want to be the strong one for my wife. I do break. Just not in front of you."

Sallie started sweeping the hardwood. "From then on, I understood him."

Some spouses will share their emotions. Some others, for whatever reasons, will not. The fact that this couple continues to walk together into their years, surrounded by friends showing grandchildren's pictures, is a testament to love and perseverance.

If a relationship is built on shallow soil, it struggles even more in loss. Many of us say the words "for better or *worse*," but most of us do not walk down the aisle, counting the worst as a reason to stay. A relationship rooted in commitment and friendship bolsters our abilities to weather the inescapable losses that come.

Ponder Point If you do not understand your partner's reaction, pause. Don't ask in the moment. Write, draw, or speak when alone what you do not understand about it. How is the response bothering or upsetting you? If so led, ask them. In Sallie's case, her answered question closed the book on the why of her husband's reaction.

You already know the soil of your relationship. Purpose to amend the fallow or nurture the good ground.

THOUGHTFUL MOMENTS

On my father's favorite place, the back patio, my mother, her children, and grands gathered. We ate dried-up casseroles so we wouldn't have to cook and could return the dishes.

As we picked through plates of cake, my brother carted a bag of golf clubs into our midst. Without saying a word, he teed up, grabbed a wood, and whacked the ball into my parents' pasture.

We all cheered and hooted. When my brother swings a golf club and connects to the ball, it is artistry.

"Who else wants to try?"

I paused from shoving Mrs. Hendrick's lemon pound cake into my mouth. "You want us to do that?"

"Come on."

My cake be darned. I needed to whack the

bounce out of something. My golf career, the shortest known to mankind, showed teenage promise, until the Sunday the truth of golf in me was revealed. Dad and I were on the ninth hole. His friends showed up.

"Go ahead, honey. Show them what you got."

Granted, I could smack a golf ball. But Dad had not counted on ratio. For every fine whack, three dribbles came. I swung, the pressure to perform far heavier than the club. After three tries, one of my dad's friends ended my misery.

"We all have bad days." Thus, my golf career came to an end.

Today would be different. This would be in memory of my father. My brother teed up the ball, then handed me the club. I rocked my feet into the soil, prayed for a perfect connection to redeem the day, refute the past. I dug my feet in, poised the club on the ground, but the club head faced backward.

"No, those are Dad's clubs. Gotta swing left-handed," my brother said.

"No way." Every weekend, my father cursed having learned to play left-handed. He vowed my baby brother, a leftie, would learn to play right. To my dad's end, he believed left-handed clubs prevented him from perfection.

"Give me a right-hand club."

"Nope. Left-handed today."

I looked at the bag. The club covers we'd all seen for years, many times having carted them to Dad's car. I looked at my brother with appreciation. What a fitting memory to create for our family.

I hit it well enough, which is to say, a dribble and a half. My siblings, nephews, nieces, and spouses, all stepped up to swing at the golf balls my brother teed up. No sacred words were spoken. Mom smiled. Our family hollered encouragements.

It was a sublime moment no one could craft. The idea popped up in my brother's mind, and here we were, on the saddest day of our life, golfing left-handed.

Ponder Point — It's sweeping, this grief. We might not feel the gratefulness of unexpected moments now. But welcome them. If appropriate, share them. The actions might become the greatest gift of the day.

IF YOUR INHERITANCE IS SEXUAL ABUSE

They were most often called the "Twins." Born a day apart during the Depression, these girls were photographed twice, once coiffed in white dresses, once holding a ball, although no one seems to remember which twin. They were identical.

The girls shared chores, hopes, and secrets. Dark ones.

Hand me-Downs

Ginned up, Grandpa tipped over table
and chairs, the lone couch in the house.
Grandma worked at the local elementary
where her twins, Liv and Lily, schooled.
After the bell rang, Liv scrubbed freezers
and floors at Bassie's Ice Cream Shop;
her wages bought family butter and bread.

At night, Papdaddy slipped into the twins'
closet to scare, crashing open the door
with a shotgun. The metal barrel
propped against Liv's bed, she hated
sounds: an undone zipper, the wrestle
of sheets, a grunt from her sister's bed,
the whisper in her head saying,
"I'm not the pretty one."

Sexual abuse leaves a history of confusion and pain so deep its hurt feels best buried.

Upon the death of their father in his late eighties, one of the twins visited his casket at the funeral home.

"I had a long talk with him," she said. "I told him he ruined us. Only an evil man would do such a thing to his girls." This woman had held her words to her father for five decades.

Even before the expected death of one, the twins never spoke of what nights held in their shared childhood. They had never mentioned it to their mother. The dying one told a daughter only. The secret was secreted away, as if in the very cedar closet their father once hid.

Many of us carry sexual abuse with us to the grave, if not theirs, to our own. This private history might instruct our lives, convoluting our marriages, causing us to hyperinflate fears for our children. This abuse becomes like another sibling in our family. There are the twins, and their constant companion, Shame.

We live and move in a world where our bone-deep hurts are carried by many, spoken by few. This is the heinous inheritance, this ugly secret.

"For there is a time and a way for everything, although man's trouble lies heavy on him."

~ Ecclesiastes 8:6 (ESV)

Ponder Point A friend of mine, a counselor, was only able to speak about the rape she'd lived through after the death of the relative. Until that point, only her husband knew.

Some of us may speak and be helped in expressing words. In the talking, the inheritance can be rewritten by some miraculous act beyond our understanding.

Some of us will never speak of this. No judgment here. This same friend recommended writing or speaking to your younger self. Tell your childhood "you" what you wished she knew then, and what you know about her now.

Whatever the case, check your life. Are you in a healthy relationship, or have you chosen one that reinforces the history bequeathed to you by an abuser?

TO HELL WITH GRIEF

The woman meandered through the building, searching for Room 217, the number assigned to the grief group. Hands clutching workbooks, eyes focused on the floor, a few women ringed the room. She wished now to take back the confession that led her here. She had blurted to her new friend, the group's leader, "I need to grieve." Waiting for her turn to introduce herself, she listened to the hurt the other women shared. Some stayed quiet.

"Apparently men don't grieve," she stated when her time came. Humor was her way.

"Our groups tend to lean towards women," her friend said. "We get the occasional man."

So much for stalling, the woman thought. She launched into her story. Tears edged her eyes. She never doubted the grief work was needed, but she was not the crying type either.

During the course's instruction, she crossed her legs, clutched her arms across her body, adjusted her seat. Her heart raced. She didn't want to be one of those people in one of those groups. She wanted to run to the door and bolt.

A participant leaned over and said, "There's a self-assessment test every week." Encouragement shined from her eyes. "The daily work will be so helpful."

Oh, joy. Reading her tax returns sounded better than rating her emotions every week. It was then this woman knew she needed to be there. The fear of pain had silenced her. She did not want to look at the past any more than she allowed herself. She did not want to ponder it, because it spoke to the future.

Granted, loss was a part of life, yet examining it only signaled that more pain was coming.

Denying grief brought her control. This group asked for submission to a process outside herself. Surrendering her tight circle of emotions was not in her mode of operation. Yet she came to understand her busyness with life and caring for the living had snuffed her grief. Her emotional and physical well-being was being compromised. More than that, her joy had been stuffed into cracks and corners of her day, if allowed light at all. The woman knew she may not want to be there, but she needed this.

In the video teaching, Zig Ziglar said, "Grief is the price we pay for loving someone."

Sandwiched between two other heavy hearts, this woman stayed because of that statement. The truth leaves no wiggle room. She had loved, and nothing, but nothing, would stop her from continuing. To hell with the fear of grieving.

Ponder Point In the 1800s, the poet, Alfred Lord Tennyson, sums up the inclination to avoid grief:

"But in my spirit will I dwell,
And dream my dream, and hold it true;
For tho' my lips may breathe adieu,
I cannot think the thing farewell."

In Memoriam A.H.H," Lord Alfred Tennyson

We may be surprised, after the tears and pain, more roads need walking. This woman did not want to commit two months to a group, but she chose to trust the process. Her way had not worked. Anxiety and worry, most especially her need for control, wore her down. She moved a step forward.

A Night at the Neighbor's Museum

A friend, Lane, was going home to an empty house. It was her first visit after the funeral. Nobody was with her. Her father and my father had worked together for years, had lived in two different neighborhoods near one another, their friendship that strong.

My childhood was filled with memories of crossing Greensboro Road, finding her mother at their kitchen buffet, reading the romances she loved. During Christmas, Mrs. B's sisters and she would set up the cardboard table and finish 1000-piece puzzles in as much time as most of us eat popcorn.

Then, Mrs. B started dying. By this time, I was wrapped up in my mom's cancer. Rarely did I stop by. Too soon, Lane's mother moved from their California King to a hospital bed.

The year before, I'd received the call my dad had passed. Even though he was eighty-five, his death came without warning. Mom was the one with cancer after all. I cried on my porch, my eyes fixed on the mighty oak tree, begging help from God. I tossed clothes in my car, the dreaded funeral ones, flung money at adult children to help the teens buy appropriate dresses, and drove the three-plus hours to my parents' house.

I paused at the subzero, where my dad had fallen. Knelt, prayed, cried. Then breathing deeply, I walked the hallway to their bedroom.

Given the time, Mom had been tucked

in by her caregiver. But her eyes shined and an inaudible sigh filled the room, saying, "I am not alone." We cried more, then I went to their bathroom to ready for sleep. For the first time, my dad's side of the sink was available. I slid open his drawer. A toothbrush, such an insignificant item, but his. I spritzed his aftershave on my wrist. The black comb hinted of his hair.

Usually, the guest room was my place. But not this night. Probably never again. This night I slept on my dad's side of the bed, unwashed sheets and all. Little did I know, but it was preparing me for the future, for my friend, Lane, and the loss of her mother.

I called Lane. "I want to come to town and stay with you."

"Really?"

My schedule could be moved, this here, that there. "Truly."

"We can sleep in Mom and Dad's room."

My heart skipped. Then, I remembered sleeping on my dad's sheets. Lane could not be alone. Not on my watch. "Sure."

After a late night catching up, I stared up at her parent's skylight as I sought sleep. Fortunately, these sheets were cleaned. The wind whipping, a zip of fear wiggled in, the same kind I had in childhood. I was afraid of the dark and what I might see within it. "Go away," I whispered, so Lane couldn't hear me. "Night, friend," I spoke so she could.

"Good night. I'm glad you're here."

Blessed sleep followed.

Ponder Point After the casseroles dry, when you visit your loved ones' house again, ask a friend to accompany you. If it is your house, ask a friend to stay the weekend. True friends will. Ask one. Be one.

BEING STILL LIKE OUR GRANDMOTHERS

The bees needed sugaring, the animals feeding, and the babies—whether small or grown—attending. Shriveled petunia blossoms wanted plucking, and energy bills paying.

Yet all I wanted was to sit on the porch, as my grandmothers before me, one in front of twin oaks, the other, twin maples. I often wondered what Mamaw and Nannie had pondered. Did they pull out their memories, reading them like a book, imagining different directions that might have led to different paths?

But my loss journey hasn't allowed inactivity. My older teens need help in navigating grief. They alternate between sadness and laughter, quick as a pendulum swing.

Added to their emotional moves, the tasks of death demand action—finding documents, answering calls, giving rundowns.

After scrubbing off the hospital, after the flowers died, I was stunned by exhaustion. The deep DNA kind that leveled me by six in the evening. "What is wrong with me?" I asked myself this question a few times, then resigned my body to fatigue, until my legs shook and my balance wavered.

I wanted normal again. I wanted to sit on the porch, see fireflies introduce summer, stay up past bedtime and read more than three paragraphs of a book before falling asleep.

I wanted more, really. Pushing the glider with my foot, I longed to sit beside Nannie, and let silence fall like sweet rain. I wanted to listen to Mamaw's rocker creak, as she turned the page of her Bible.

I, the caregiver, wanted to be cared for, to be mothered or fathered, although they have passed, as my grandmothers have.

Recognizing this "want" helped. I needed help. My memories were not adequate nurturing. But I could slip into a bath, warming my cold muscles. I could rely on paninis and omelets as dinner. I could gather the teens in the early evenings, each of us speaking our day's outcome. Eat fresh blueberries with whipped cream. Pray by my bed.

The sun slipping near the horizon, I could sit in my chair outside and stare at the weeping willows while the breeze shimmered the pond.

Ponder Point When exhaustion feels like a layer of skin, you might want to consider a good porch sit. Being quiet and still, like my grandmothers did, helps evaporate the façade that the whole world is in your hands. Rest a spell, they would say.

Later, delegate. Find point people in your family, friendships, and organizations to disseminate needed information to you or to pass communication along. If immediate family members step up to be points of contact, make sure they are the wise choice—people who will give the information only, and not private details or other unnecessary information.

Ask a trusted friend to either help with monthly bills or serve as a reminder. If that's not possible, rate the bills in order of importance and do only the necessary for that day. After this be still again, if only for a few moments.

WATCHING OUR YOUNG ADULTS GRIEVE

My young adult daughter sits low on the kitchen stepping stool. Born in Asia to Asian parents, she has this squat unique to that part of the world. It is a buttocks-touching-ankle movement that does not show up in Anglo-Saxon DNA and can result in pinched muscles if attempted. I should know.

She squats as I prepare a simple dinner, as I have no energy to go further than hamburger and scrambled eggs.

"Mom, a girl from church has died."

"Oh, no," I say once, the unspoken being the parents. Dear God, the parents. Being new to the church, I recall the people I know and prepare my heart, as several have young adults and teens.

"She committed suicide." Forensic-oriented, my daughter searches media, examining the friends of hers, studying the young woman's posts. Her face was excited with Senior Prom. Her dress and hair and makeup were fairytale. Her young escort had rented a limo. The photographs told the story of Beloved Princess.

My daughter studied the wondrous face for hints of the tragedy to come, but none were noticeable in early spring. By midsummer, pain of such magnitude had occurred to push this young woman to the edge.

I wondered if I'd passed her along the way to Sunday School or in the bathroom. I hoped, if I did, I said, "Hello." I wondered about her friends, how they were coping, such an idiotic phrase in these moments.

We, as seasoned adults, can barely hold it together. My daughter struggled to even know where to begin. Entering the room, her younger sibling pounced on us. She entreated us for answers to unrelated matters, ignoring our somber tone.

"Can you please just stop?" my older asked my younger.

"Be gentle with your sister tonight," I reminded my hyperactive teen. "She's sad."

She continued to ping pong from emotion to emotion.

"Calm down." I grasped her around the shoulders. "Stop. We're concerned about a family. It's their worst time ever."

She glanced at her hurting sister and grabbed me in a rare hug.

I held her tight. "I love you, my daughter."

Ponder Point Watching another person's pain pile up faster than a snowstorm hurts. We carry not only our grief and calamity, the what ifs and whys, but attempt to take theirs as well. Part of letting our children grow up is acknowledging they must experience hard times along with the happy ones.

Teens and young adults handle bad news differently. Their pain is no less. They are simply tracking on a different issue. Ask them to give you a timeout. Earmark a certain time when you will address their concerns. Ask them to remind you. Prepare to respond.

A wise counselor said, "Remember, you are the parent. They are the child." No matter how old they are.

How is your journey with your young adults and teens today?

WHO WANTS DAD'S IGUANA?

Everyone admired Dad's love of all creatures great and small. Unfortunately, being handed a loved one's barn of horses, aquarium of slithering creatures, or herd of dogs or cats, was not figured into the plan upon his death.

Extended family might step up to care for them temporarily. But long-term decisions must be made. In some instances, the animal is taken by a family member. Many are routed to shelters where lifespans are numbered in single digits. Some animals end up on social websites. Some are abandoned.

Harder still is making the decision of what to do with the beloved creature. We did not ask for this problem. We wished our loved ones had thought this through. But here we are, surrounded by six gerbils, while a German Shepherd paces in the next room. Dander, the feedings, and scooping poop are new additions to overloaded emotions.

Domestic animals grieve too. They do not understand the changes. They will not understand being left overnight without their routine or loved one. On top of this, the animal may not act normally, needing to adjust. If a loved one's animal remains or is aggressive, a vet can determine the best course of action to take.

Acclimating an animal to a new home or routine takes time. Finding the perfect familial fit for a loved one's animal takes vetting. Having to make hard choices adds to our overloaded stress levels. We must be wary of snap decisions. A shelter should not be an option. If possible, we should consider adopting our loved one's animal. My rescue dog turned into the best of canines and even saved me from being hit by an old oak tree.

My daughter's rescue cat is her beloved animal. My other daughter has rescued two German Shepherds, who are part of their family lore. Adoption is not an overnight process, but one well worth the commitment.

Ponder Point In the early 2000s, Leona Helmsley, famed for her boutique hotels and use of pumpkin orange, left $12 million to the care of her beloved dog, Trouble. It was such a fabulous story, it made news then. Now millions of Americans, average and wealthy, have included their animals in their end-of-life planning.

Yet most animals are not considered. If your loved one left this task up in the air, their care falls to the family. This is tough work, and the solutions are often difficult.

Ask for help. Ask for plenty of help. Make sure the animals are current on their necessary shots.

If your loved one has farm animals, ask the teenage farmer next door. If your loved ones had close friends who visited often, solicit their aid, as the animals will be comforted by familiar scents and voices. Ask the animal's vet. Ask their church or organizations for help.

If the animals are safe, employ older children to help in feedings, to throw a ball, or take the animal out for a walk.

In the meanwhile, if family members can't take the animals, reach out to the same trusted groups. Check and verify the homes willing to adopt Fido. In the grief of letting an animal go, remember the joy they will provide for their new family.

Plan in your own will a succession of care for your animals. Do not leave this to your loved ones, who will be working through enough without this added duty.

DEATH IMPACTS
THE YOUNG:
WE JUST DON'T SEE IT

Fifty years ago, the backsides of televisions were very complicated, unlike today. A tube of electronic genius was stationed there, along with protruding hardware and a panel of small holes that glowed. All this brought my family was animal kingdoms, outer space, and the Grand Ole Opry.

I hid behind the television after my mother cried on the telephone. My cousin, actually a second-generation, had been a passenger in a dune buggy. His hair would not have whipped in the wind. Great Aunt Opal made sure his was short and glued in place. But his eyes would have brightened at the new experience, the thrill of speed.

Jeffrey was the cousin who listened to me, who paid attention even though I was considerably younger at the time. He performed his magic tricks for us, making a penny disappear in his palm. He played an accordion, and rivaled Creedence Clearwater Revival as the coolest.

"He's not going to make it?" My mother's voice pitched as never before. "He's too young."

Jeffrey was sixteen. The favorite person in my young world, my cousin visited sparingly, living towns away, only adding to his mystique. He was the kindest. He did not treat me like older teens who either ignored or underestimated me.

Behind the TV, ignoring my mother's soap opera, I inhaled the television chemical as I sobbed.

Days later, I wrote Jeffrey a note. I hunted my mother's tiny Bible she'd carried her wedding day and found a verse. I copied it for him. Aunt JoAnne tucked the notebook paper beside him in his casket.

My life pivoted that day. Old people died, not my cousin whom I loved and delighted in. Despite remembering the live news coverage when Robert Kennedy was assassinated, feeling the horror at an early age, wondering why Mom pointed her finger for me to leave the room, this struck a million times more.

I loved God and going to Mr. Riley's Sunday School class. I loved the flannel board the missionaries used to teach stories at my school. I loved sitting in nature and counting the number of petals on a daisy.

"All their life in this world and all their adventures in Narnia had only been the cover and the title page: now at last they were beginning Chapter One of the Great Story which no one on earth has read: which goes on forever: in which every chapter is better than the one before."

~ CS Lewis, *The Last Battle*

When I examined my life, two decades ago, I realized how momentous Jeffrey's death was to my faith and me. I was the running joke in my family. When we were driving to the beach, a while after his passing, we took a shortcut through a small town. A coffin was being carried out of a church.

"Who died?" I asked all my people in our old brown station wagon.

The front seat started laughing first, then thereafter, all my siblings down to the youngest. I had to giggle as well. It was a silly question with a serious want-to-know.

Death became a haunt of mine. I chose to erase it with alcohol and guys, to ignore it by closing my white Bible for the last time at sixteen. I doubted everybody yet allowed danger into my life. Most of my unsavory actions in my late teens and throughout my early twenties pointed back to the emotional hurt I held, from losing my most important person in life to death.

Ponder Point Don't underestimate the effects of death, even if they are not constant loved ones in the lives of your children. Ask your young about their hurts. Do not treat the talk like a once-and-done. This conversation should be on-going throughout their lives, offered up in wisdom of the When and the What. You are the Who, however. Don't push it aside. Pursue your children, tenderly. Recognize they might act out or withdraw.

BEING SCATTERBRAINED: GETTING TO KNOW YOUR LOCAL FIRE DEPARTMENT

I don't like microwaves. Every morning, the oat milk for my coffee is heated in my Chantel 3.5-quart pot on the gas stove, then poured into my coffee with chocolate overtones.

Of late, I've walked away from cooking milk or sautéed meals. My fire alarms have been tested in real time. The latest friendship I've cultivated, with much humility and shame, is with the Pleasant Garden Fire Department. As a payback for their five visits, I've invited them to fish my pond for bass.

Similarly, driving is an issue. Since I make many calls a day, it seemed logical to use drive time for this. This action multiplied into incorporating the map while making calls. Eyes and mind are preoccupied. Driving has become agenda-oriented, rather than destination-focused.

Being pulled into many directions, being scatterbrained is normal after a loss. We find ourselves wandering

"The glory of light cannot exist without its shadows. Life is a whole, and good and ill must be accepted together. The journey has been enjoyable and well worth making—once."

~ Winston Churchill

from room to room, forgetting why we entered. Fine. Not so much when we leave the stove or perhaps a child alone. We can become anything but safe.

Living through the emotions of losing a loved one seems like enough for this day. Unfortunately, we do not have that luxury. The safety of loved ones and road strangers is our responsibility. Maturity in the time of sorrow sounds like a movie we do not want to live.

Being alert during the post-loss stage requires discipline. That very word seems cruel to mention in the weeks and months after the funeral. But we are the grownups.

Someone's life might depend upon it.

Ponder Point We will quickly identify the lapses in our judgment. If we don't, others will. Be grateful another pair of eyes are helping. Ask for tips on what to do about your potentially harmful actions.

SYMPATHY CARDS:
A FUNNY STORY

My daughters, both eleven and recently adopted from China, were thrilled to hand me my Mother's Day card. They had searched for the right one to buy in the store, my husband reported, taking hours.

I admired the beauty of the envelope, their sweet handwriting newly learned, labeling me as "Mother." I snagged my finger under the flap, opening it inch by inch, pulled the card out with a theatrical flourish boosting their anticipation.

A beautiful lavender card with an embossed lily was revealed. Across the top, in the lightest, most flourishing script read, "In Sympathy."

I could not help it. But I busted a laugh. The faces of my sweet children registered shock.

My limited acting skills were employed, and I held the card close to my heart and smiled, hoping hearts showed up in my eyes.

As I read the card further, offering me the deepest heartfelt concerns, thoughts and wishes, the laughter could no longer be held. I doubled over hooting.

"Mom, what wrong?" Linking verbs had not yet met her grammar.

"Did you read this before buying it?" I asked my husband.

"It looked pretty. I figured it was a Mother's Day card." These were code words. The fishing department had held his attention while my daughters examined and debated the best card for me.

I pulled it together, hugging them both,

joyful in their delight and the oxymoron of the moment. I added their card to my older daughter's earlier propensity to buy me funeral flowers for Mother's Day. O, to the market geared toward helping us journey through grief. Never did their bottom line anticipate a secondary market being children for Mother's Day.

Years later, after the back-to-back losses of my parents, I received sympathy cards. Four years after the passing of my first parent, my daughter who enjoys sorting mail, came to me.

"Mom, can I open these cards?"

I looked at the return addresses. They came from my parents' hometown.

"No. Put them in a file with my name on it."

"But I like opening all the mail, Mom." My daughter had suggested she become my much-needed assistant.

"Not those."

I dearly appreciated the cards, without a doubt. I looked at the names on the envelopes and thought about each person who sent one. But I am still not ready to open them, even five years later.

Ponder Point Some of us will rush to open the cards sent. My mother was. She received comfort in the words, the long or short notes, the artful cards.

Some of us are not ready. Many might say we are in denial, or not letting go, or not properly grieving because the cards remain unopened. The time will come. Feeling no pressure frees. Don't sweat the sympathy cards.

In time, be mindful of the paperwork inheritance we leave our children.

WE HAVE THIS IN COMMON

Death, like pregnancy or work, is a common denominator between people. Speak to a small group about the loss, lilies, or limousines, and everyone nods, then adds their stories.

"I lost my parents, then my sister." Lauren's southern accent softens. "My husband died the next year. That was it."

"It was my daughter for me," Gerry says.

Jackie adds, "They found my brother in his garage after three days."

It's not an attempt to outdo one another. The ground we travel during these conversations is sacred, the act of telling of our history without the bursts of emotion.

"My dad died, then Mom. We moved. My marriage failed." This woman journals, speaks or prays almost every trouble in her life. She pulls apart scenarios, examining how a situation could be made better for future use. "I need counseling."

Our minds, it seems, are conditioned to cataloging events, sorting them into their proper places. But death upends our normal patterns. We have no filing system for this loss. We either respond in attention or tuck it away.

"I don't cry." The woman states the words as a boundary, or the truth. It is unclear. "Maybe one tear." No mascara shed here.

"Might be good for you," another woman says. For years, she carried grief for her homeland, decimated by a category-five hurricane. She had wanted to fly over, but

"May mercy, peace and love be multiplied to you."

~ Jude 1:2 (ESV)

no planes could land in the flooded airport. Thirty feet of ocean covered her island. She had stayed on a calling app for days receiving reports of the missing and dead. "I still need to go home."

Something happens when we gather and open ourselves to the stories. A hand is held. A heart feels loved. A person is heard. Although the story does not change, we are reminded we are not alone.

Ponder Point We stand on common ground. Talk to a stranger in the checkout line, the teller at the window, the person in the park. We've all loved and lost, as the Bard wrote. There's nothing earth-shattering here. The magic begins when you allow yourself to join in.

VOLUNTEERING TO WALK THROUGH THE SHADOW OF DEATH

As a volunteer, Shanda bears witness to death every day.

At a celebration for a young woman, I caught Shanda's eye. She was smiling but talking very little and not being her engaging self. After I'd made visits with the other women, I approached her.

"Let's take a walk." I handed her a bottle of water.

"Yes. Let's."

We ambled down the sidewalk to the sunset. "What's up?" I asked.

"I live in two worlds."

The sunset colored the sky. I lifted my face to its beauty. A gnat bit the tar out of my leg. Yes, indeed, we live between beauty and pain.

"It's so hard to enjoy life, when the ugly is so ugly." Shanda scuffed her sandal on the driveway. "I'm not even trying to hide it anymore. I don't even think I can."

Being a cheerleader, even encouraging her at this point, was not what she needed, not going to help. This was not even about venting. It was so much more than that. This was a profound philosophical moment when death, for this moment, was winning. This was a dirge.

One definition of dirge from the Oxford Lexicon is "a mournful song, piece of music, or poem." At times like these, our cries are written on our hearts, sung or unsung because our voices cannot contain the weight.

As Shanda spoke, the sun neared the horizon, the gnats amped up their dinner selection, and a certain amount of peace was found by voicing death into the atmosphere.

The situation had not changed. Death still bored down upon her. But hope rose, as the sunrise on the other part of the world. It sounds idyllic. The fight for peace never is. It was a deep wrestling with a constant we live with every day. The phone call. The doctor's report. The innocent lane change.

Yet somehow in the speaking or silence, we come out on the other side. If only for that moment. Hope in darkness. We are between two worlds.

Ponder Point The ancient speaker and writer Paul said, "Our hope for you is unshaken, for we know that as you share in our sufferings, you will also share in our comfort."

We are gifted with many ways to walk with this deep hurt. In the speaking, comfort, however it happens, can come. It might be in music or silence. It might be in the sunset. It might be a friend willing to endure gnats to stand with you. It doesn't erase the death. But it reaches the other part of our divided heart and gives us a moment of respite.

Don't retell the story you've told hundreds of times. The details, the timeline, the visuals. Speak the hurt. Speak your dirge out loud.

SOMETIMES IT'S JUST
FOR A SEASON

Through my fields, William rode with me in the Ford. I had owned a farm for a month. Making a three-hour roundtrip, he had come to assure me the tall grass would get cut for hay. The last thing I wanted was acres of yard.

"This is a nice property." William was older than my son, but he reminded me of him. Strong, encouraging, seeing potential. A heart to teach, a heart to help.

"But will it work? This Farm Link thing?"

"You'll have more than enough farmers wanting to lease for hay." He glanced away. "I'm right here, going to help."

Help me, he did. In no time, he created an online profile for the farm, complete with excellent photography and writing,

then posted the land for hay leasing on the statewide farm link. I had farmer after farmer calling me. William was doing more than his job as Co-Director of NCFarmLink. He was doing what he loved, connecting landowners with farm producers.

Throughout the following two years, I would call him every now and then. Checking varieties for the new orchard or the possibility of squeezing timber into my acreage. We would catch up on children. I would remind him how quick it all goes. He would agree.

Five days before his death, William stood on my property, prepared to participate in a video on North Carolina's great opportunities for land use and farming. I was to be included in the video with the farmers who lease my land. Instead, I was in Charlotte with a hospitalized family member.

"Sorry about what you're going through," William told me over the phone.

Always such a kind young man, William loved his family and loved to help people. He always knew how or what to do or found someone who did. I will never forget how a stranger went out of his way to help this woman, who feared owning a hundred-acre lawn, and from that, a friendship began. More than that, William had reminded me of the intricacies and preciousness of our food source. Emphasizing the generational beauty of the farming community, he encouraged and aided many people to continue their family's legacy.

William was that kind of man.

Ponder Point The longer we live, the more stories we gain of people passing. Some individuals come into our lives for only a season; people we cannot forget. They might guide us through difficult and uncertain times. They might bring us laughter and stories. Then suddenly, they're gone. We miss knowing they are in the world, making it a better place.

Consider reaching out to their families to bless them as you have been blessed by them.

Getting by with a Little Help from My Friends

I was beat. I pushed off grief for my father due to my mother's dire health concerns. Then I stuffed mourning for my mother to a later date because of a loved one's chronic disease and estate matters.

Unfortunately, an accident left the loved one in severe trauma, needing much attention, out of town. Intense meetings, requiring multiple trips, also took place out of town. I'd noticed the last time I'd driven home I treated my car as an office, calling people, pulling over for texts, abstract thinking. In other words, I was not present. In a major city, I drifted into another lane.

I had become dangerous.

To correct this on the hour commute to the Charlotte hospital, I promised to keep my cell away, not change radio channels, nor script notes. The problem came when being the advocate meant being available for a call, wherever I might be. Car or no car. In this case, I waited for insurance's approval of an appeal after a rehab hospitalization had been denied for my loved one. I drove home holding my cell, not knowing what we would do if he was not approved to go to the facility. I could not miss that call.

I shared my fears with my friend, Laura, asking for prayer. She did that, and even one better. "Let me help. I'll drive you."

"No, no. I can handle this." It is better to give than receive, I'd learned. I was comfortable with the former, skin-crawling at the latter.

"Why don't you let me? I'm totally free," my friend said. "I want to do this."

Why could I not accept? Of course. I was the one who handled events. I was the one to help others. In the examination of my soul, I realized I was not only depriving another of doing good but turning down the very help needed. Because of my control issue. I wanted to be the one to help. I wanted to be the strong one.

In short, hello, my ego. Meet your emotional defect.

"I have a lot of calls to make."

My friend knows me. She remained silent to let me speak it.

"On the way back home, I inched into another lane."

She waited.

"So many calls need to be made."

My thoughts waded through the hours after the loved one's ICU psychosis, multiple doctors' visits, trays of liquids, nurses' shifts. The exhausted trek up the stairs in the parking garage at night. I dared to ask more. "Can you stay the night in the hotel with me?"

I'd stayed overnight enough on this loved one's behalf to know what hotel room we could get. My friend would be comfortable there as I went to the hospital. I could avoid sitting at the restaurant alone, book open, left unread. I would skip flipping channels and never landing.

My friend waited.

"Yes, I need help. Desperately."

My ego was put to rest, yet another kind of rest came, one of mind, body, spirit. No, indeed, I was not alone.

Ponder Point Friends want to help. It's hard to receive. Consider the blessing they and you are missing by your stubbornness or fear of imposing. Consider the danger your exhaustion might bring to others. Say yes to help.

WE ARE HISTORY

A disease spread across one country after another until the world felt its presence. Fear reigned. Families were divided, quarantining from one another in distant places. The breeze seemed to shout, "run, run, run," as if speed and isolation would save. Yet the disease haunted and hunted, finding those who had kept themselves "safe," and sparing some who'd entered the fray. Money could not solve it. Governments were left in shambles. People were breathless waiting for the next wave to steal a family member.

This was the mid-1300s, the time of the Black Plague, a bacterial infection. One-third of Europe died.

"May I say to you that you will find that the bravest of men have been those who have been afraid. May I also say that all of us experience something that fills our hearts with fear."

~ Dr. J. Vernon McGee

In 1918, the Spanish Flu skipped over my grandmother's house, but left every neighbor surrounding her burying a loved one. Virgie Mae Fleenor, my Mamaw, was seventeen years old, and hoping to become a teacher, a wife, and mother. Even to this day, her large family holds a family reunion. These survivors of multiple epidemics, wars, the Great Depression, recessions, and presidents were the family patriarchs and matriarchs.

Hiking my pasture, I stamped thirsty

ground with my walking stick, carried to ward off copperheads. Afterwards, I took the trash out, and in the mundane, all hell broke. I hunkered near a sixty-year-old tree and sobbed. No matter that my decades are many, I wanted my mom and my dad. I was exhausted from all the praying for acquaintances, friends, and strangers. Even as white clouds flitted across blue sky, I wondered when my God was going to move.

The juxtaposition of life and death is grasped by our minds and hearts daily. None of us get out of life alive. Personal tragedies couple with local, national, and even worldwide ones, to overwhelm us, literally to death at times. The veil between this world, and whatever comes after, stretches thin as gauze over a body.

We live the history that passes away.

Ponder Point

Sleep

Aunt Fretta's grave had caved.
Soil blanketed the mother and
stillborn babe she delivered.
Nannie wove us around dead
loved ones behind Lime Hill.
I was young and taught that day
to circle graves, not cross them.
Grannie Sug's husbands flanked her—
Van Hook to the left, Hosea, the right.
Full of spit and vinegar, Sug
taught my daddy to Lindy Hop
before heading to war.

Jagged granite peppers the berm
in my yard. Twice a year for two
decades, I have shaken pine bales here.
This year, the pattern shown: four in a row,
six in a line, three on the crest, several alone—
rock as headstones,
where dogwood and red buds sprout,
living their decades, if not ill.

I dreamed a white farmhouse with pine
planked floors. I opened the backdoor,
expecting pasture for Angus, patches of oak.
Instead, tombstones sprang from spring hills.

A Florentine man wrote that people
were layered like lasagna in mass
graves during the Bubonic Plague.
The virus, I read, sleeps soil deep,
dreaming.

THE YEAR THE COLORS CHANGED

Jack stared at the picture of his dad on the table. It was just another morning until his mom poured the milk.

"It's orange!"

'Yes, son. It's that kind of year."

Jack stirred Toasty Marsh-mallow Squares in his bowl. "I want my old milk back."

"Hurry up. School." Mom put the jug in the fridge.

Jumping the steps out-side, Jack ran his hands through a mist floating by. "Mom, it's red like your church dress."

"Yes, it is."

Morning light peeked over the neighbor's gray house. "The sun's purple!"

"You have your lunch?"

Jack rubbed his sneakers across the blue grass. A pink mouse hopped over his toes.

What was going on? Everything was mixed up. Even the sky was wild. "It's green?"

"Son, it's been that kind of year."

Jack would have liked to color this world on his big, drawing paper. He didn't like living in it.

On the way to school, he thumped his shoe against the front seat. The spring trees

"….in the smallest matters of life, bring everything before God, the little things, the very little things, what the world calls trifling things…"

~ L.B. Cowman

were striped like candy canes. "When will it go back to the way it was?"

Mom tapped the steering wheel, the thing she did when she was thinking. She had done that a lot. "Honey, it's not."

"It's been that kind of year." Jack was tired of his mom saying that, so he said it for her.

"It's been hard."

"It's upside-down." Jack pretended to paint the trees green.

"We're still a family."

"Dad and I never did T-ball."

"No, you didn't."

Jack didn't like the sound of his mom's voice. "But Grandpa plays it with me."

"It's not the same, is it?"

"Grandpa's better at playing in his garden."

"Remember what Pastor Dan said?"

Pastor Dan said a lot, Jack thought.

"We need to trust God," Mom said.

"That's hasn't changed anything."

Mom adjusted the car mirror. She was thinking again. "I talk to him when I feel that way."

"What do you say?"

"I tell him I don't like this."

"You tell him that, Mom?"

"Yep. But I remind myself He's got this, even if I don't get it."

"You believe that?"

"I'm trying."

"He has the blue grass?"

Mom nodded yes.

"He has the purple sun?"

She nodded again.

"He has the green sky?"

"He's got that too."

"No matter if I like it or not?"

Mom turned down the long driveway to Hope Street Elementary.

"This trust stuff"—Jack blew out his breath—"is hard work."

"Yes, yes, it is."

"I liked it the old way." Jack grabbed his backpack. "I'll try."

"Good man."

"Dad used to say that."

He could tell Mom wanted to say something because she kept swallowing. She pulled into school.

Principal Adams waved good morning. Today was pizza day, Jack's favorite day of the week. He smiled at his friends.

Some things hadn't changed. Marco still liked climbing trees. Trish still helped him with math. Zach still like dodge ball.

"I'm happy God gave me you." Mom blew him a kiss like she did every day.

"He's got us, Mom." Even if the colors stayed mixed up.

It had been that kind of year.

Ponder Point We feel like children. Color. Draw. Color with your children or grands.

Don't hide your hurts from them. However, be discerning on the details you give. Lean on someone stronger.

Thank You Notes,
No Thank You

Can we admit thank you notes are a curse to some of us who have lost loved ones?

My mother, God bless her soul, bought me a monogrammed cream paper and envelope writing kit early in my twenties. From gift tags to thank you notes, to deeper letters requiring more writing space, the fancy box was filled. Four decades later, I still house this stationery in a drawer, waiting for the perfect moment to bestow the wonder and beauty of my initials and verbiage upon someone.

Admittedly, this accessory has come in handy in a pinch for graduations, weddings,

"Wisdom is good with an inheritance, an advantage to those who see the sun."

~ Ecclesiastes 7:11 (ESV)

even birthday checks. When my father passed, my precious sister-in-hearts stepped in and wrote perfect notes to people I did not know. After my mother passed, I employed a bit of my stationery with a few of Mom's friends, yet my sisters once again wrote the many. What a gift.

During grieving, many of us rise to the thank you note call. My friend Robin hand-crafts cards of such artistry. Another friend finds the writing soothing and cathartic.

Others of us would like to speak to the inventor of the concept. The upside-down nature of thanking people for showing sympathy to our families rather screams illogic for some of us.

Emily Post Etiquette (emilypost.com, Different Ways to Say Thank-You) states the rule for sympathy notes:

"Send a written thank-you to anyone who sent a personal note, flowers or a donation. It's fine for a close friend or relative to write notes on the recipient's behalf."

We acknowledge the correctness of thank you cards. But we cannot muster up the energy to add another to-do to our grieving hearts. We are weary of asking family members for yet one more help. Where does this leave us, those who are thankful, but thankless in writing?

Ponder Point If you missed the use of acknowledgement cards provided by funeral homes, a friend with a graphics bent can design a note of thanks. A homemade digital note can be emailed. At the risk of etiquette upheaval, this might be the best we can manage. Given time later, one can write or call.

Whatever you do, if you run into my mother in heaven, God rest her soul, please don't tell her about this.

THE FIRST HOLIDAY

Great Uncle Macon was a newspaper editor, the kind seen in the black and white movies, a cigar-smoking, whiskey-drinking man. He lived big as his laugh. After imbibing too much, he would get serious. Questions chewed at his soul. Then one day, he was no more.

Much to my father's dismay, the only dress I had brought to the funeral had a large stain. Unfortunately, the only other clothing option I had packed were dress shorts. In the 80s, these were fashionable, but not at a funeral. Given we were expected at the church in an hour, I had no other choice. As we walked down the aisle, I attempted to blend into the family. The bewilderment on my cousins' faces pointed to the sorry state of my outfit. Something told me Great Uncle Macon would have liked my houndstooth shorts, at his funeral no less.

As Christmas neared, I was troubled by Great Aunt Letty and my cousin spending the holiday alone, without their husband and dad.

"You two come spend Christmas with us," I told Aunt Letty on the phone.

"I couldn't do that." Her Georgia accent twanged extra.

"Do you want to spend Christmas there?"

She did not answer, a bona fide oddity in her case. She, like Macon, lived loud. Her words "su-ga" and "hon-ee" were overheard a county over. Every room she entered, she owned, not by her design, but by the way she was designed. Our Marilyn Monroe, only older. No better way to describe her.

"No, I don't."

I was a freshman in college. Only after the

asking did I consider that I should have con- sulted with my parents first. The Christmas season was the busiest and most social time of their year.

"We can't do that," Mom said.

"They need to be alone," Dad replied, meaning he did not want to see their pain. Deep down, past the layers of grouch, my dad was tender, especially about death.

"We can't un-invite them, Frank," my mom said.

Christmas morning, we gathered on my parents' twin couches. Coffee and gifted gingerbread from their friends started the morning sweet. I glanced around us all together, very proud of my work when the unexpected happened.

It was utter and complete silence.

I looked at my talkative sister who twisted her scarf. Aunt Letty turned her head to the side, away from us. My cousin grabbed her mother's hand. I long to say something to end the awkwardness, but here it was, upon us.

What had I done? I nudged Mom to say something, and she nudged Dad. After more minutes, my crossed leg stopped tapping. "This has to be hard."

Something broke open. Acknowledging the pain, a first holiday brings, loosened us up. Each one of us recalled a story of Great Uncle Macon, his way of doing things. We learned special things he did for Letty and my cousin. His memory was honored as they remembered the love.

We had unwrapped gifts without one of them being physical. The remembrance of his presence was all the presents we needed.

Ponder Point Holidays haunt. The first one takes us by surprise. If people offer, join them.

If you know of someone who's recently lost a loved one, be the one to invite. That was one of my most special Christmases, happening over forty years ago. Life-giving memories still come from that time, particularly now that my parents are gone.

SHAME ON ME:
UNFORGIVEN ACTS

One too many ruffles on his tux, Kevin picked me up in his mother's Porsche. His acne had flared. We were silent for ten minutes while he drove us to a Chinese buffet. I had found a peach prom dress that complimented my tennis tan. The wrist corsage was going to bug me all night.

"Got anything to drink?" I asked.

"You're just a freshman."

"I have a fake ID."

Sweat streaked his face. Kevin should have taken his jacket off to drive. "I'm not sure."

"We need something to drink."

The Porsche eased to a stop at a light. "Just a little bit."

Kevin pulled the contraband alcohol from his tux. I snatched the bottle, drinking straight from it, offering him half after I was finished. My heels clapping around his car, I fell into the passenger seat, breathless, delighting in the cherry-vodka buzz and my wildness. That is the last I remember of my first prom, that and hearing his plea to not hop out the door and circle the car again at the stoplight.

At school, I avoided him. A good friend pulled me aside. "His sister feels like you used him. To go to the prom."

"I'd never do that."

"Then talk to him."

I never did. The following year, he drove his mother to a hospital in the Porsche and wrecked. My friend implored me to go with her to the funeral home. We stopped by, in the off hours. Two coffins lined the mauve room. His sister was the only other person there. She did not speak to me. She should not have. As my friend offered comfort, I backed against the door.

"I'm sorry." My parting words to her were sincere, but too much had happened to make them believable.

This was forty and some years ago.

When a person we love, we have known, or we have connected with dies, our minds do not only grieve, but surprisingly, unearth other emotions. Memories of mistakes and missed opportunities, the stubbornness of our souls, are often brought to light. The wooden boxes and metal urns pound our defenses. Shame reigns.

We can stuff the memories that bring sharp knives to our guts. Or we can purpose to ask for forgiveness.

I would have liked Kevin to have lived. I wished I would have gotten to know him. I wished drinking had not been part of that night, as his life turned to partying after that. I would have liked to have apologized for my heinous behavior. I would like, to this day, to connect with his sister and tell her how very sorry I am.

Ponder Point Unforgiveness will linger in your soul. Before approaching a surviving loved one, seek wise counsel. Check your motives. This will not be a quick fix.

Are you only doing this to make yourself feel better? Is this for the healing of the other person? Would it be best to confess to God, a close friend, or a letter never sent? If you get the green light, move forward in forgiveness. Don't push off today what you'll forget tomorrow.

STUCK AS A CRITTER IN THE POOL FILTER

Unable to fall asleep, I lifted my hand to the ceiling. Too much traveled my mind, from my mother's cancer for twelve years, a loved one's Parkinson's disease, and another's mental illness, a teenage pregnancy, two adoptions, the family business, grandchildren born, a house move, a near death experience. All the major stressors of life checked and double checked.

Earlier that day, I'd cleaned my pool traps, shaking out a dead frog. No doubt the frog swam and leapt to get out of the trap until he could no longer. I understood. I lifted my hand in surrender. I am stuck.

"I'm so tired." I could see no way forward, but through pain and more pain. "I'm so tired." Gratefully, minute hopes of laughter surrounded my life, between a tween grandchild, a grandbaby, a walk through the pasture, a row in the pond.

Turning to my side, I asked for good breathing, and no gasping, in sleep and an unclenched jaw. That was all I asked.

When had my dreams died with my loved ones? Joy had been overwhelmed and fled. When had hope hopped a train for the coast with the "three men I admire most, The Father, Son and the Holy Ghost?"

I'd talked it out, prayed it out, cried it out, walked it out, shopped it out, ate it out, stressed it out. I even scaled the wall and cleared it. But here I landed and here I stood. Muck stuck as the blue heron we had to rescue from the water's edge after a deluge.

The realization comes, and to say it's not frightening is a lie. I cannot change this. I cannot run from this. I cannot help my children or grands or friends. I cannot even help myself. I have this minute to live. Then the next and the next until my end.

I want to take a drug. Drink whiskey. Eat cake. Cuss a blue streak. Rend clothing. Anything to numb the waiting, the wading through the stuck.

"An inheritance gained hastily in the beginning will not be blessed in the end."

~ Proverbs 20:21 (ESV)

No, dear ones, we do not do this. We walk ourselves through these things. No drug, no whiskey, no cake, no cussing, or rending will help. The one part of our bodies that seems to work fine is our logic and our awareness. We are stuck and nothing, but nothing, will unstick us.

My belief will carry me, but life will never be the same. It burns.

Ponder Point Breathe. I have nothing more than that. Take deep breaths. You're not alone, but these words, we spit out. Blessings upon you, dear one.

Bob Marley Was Right

For years and months now, my family and I have journeyed barefoot down the gravel road of grief.

The pitstops are present, the numb, the reality checks, the paper chase, the what ifs, the missing person at the family event.

Last night, I dropped into a chair on the patio and marveled over the multicolored coneflowers, the blue hydrangea that was not there last year.

Voices were overheard. Then my daughters curved along the flower bed, walking with their Chinese teacher, now friend, from Hong Kong. Their Chinese teacher, called Laoshi, has followed them through their tweens, teens and now, twenties.

Gesturing, they spoke about subjects I was not privy to. They circled toward the field, Tinkerbell the dog bounding with them on their trek.

Calm and peace covered over an anxiety I held tight without knowing. Would my children be okay?

Through the walnut tree planted sixty years ago, past the butterfly bushes, the sunset started its warm descent. The girls stalled their walk, as they contemplated the granite nature embedded along the path.

I smiled. My girls, my young women, my other adult children were going to be fine after I passed. A deep knowing threaded my soul. Something bigger was at work here, not dependent on me.

Several years ago, I reached out to my dearest friends' daughters. No longer the little princesses, I wanted to get to know them as teens. It was quite unintentional at first, starting as a carpool, growing into gatherings and event goings. We would text new writers on our wish lists and reviews of books read. We talked about sex and guys. We talked about the future. Conversations were soaked in honesty and pursuit of truth.

Then, I started inviting others into my daughters' lives. A woman, who had lived in sixteen foster homes, and was a teenage mom, graduated college, and became an entrepreneur, spends an hour each week with both daughters. A wise woman, born on the islands, who lived a different childhood, connects with them regularly. Another, who had mentored an older child of mine, encourages the youngest. Still another stepped in and sacrificed her summer to help one in a school subject. This is a sampling of their network of mentoring women.

Grateful to all the mentors who had come alongside my children, I leaned back in my chair, and experienced deep rest. God and I smiled together. Long, long, long after I'm gone, my children will benefit from the most precious legacy left to them: friendships.

Ponder Point Even our youngest of children, when surrounded by vetted, loving people, can be encouraged to grow in knowing they are not alone. When your children are old enough, support mentorship in your home, from coloring books to cooking Chinese food or talking about career paths. We parents model the practice of seeking wise counsel and can help them to a network of others that will linger past our lifetimes.

Ultimately, we pass on a legacy of attitude to our children. Yes, this world is far from ideal, and the groans of life find us all. Yet, throughout the ages, poets to historical legends have written how one precious memory has carried the day.

Imagine for one Bob Marley moment, the rising sun bringing a smile to your face, then three little birds landing in front of you, adding their sweet song. It's going to be all right.

COME BACK SOON

A relative fought a long battle with her mother whose body had been invaded by a brutal cancer. This disease was labeled terminal from the onset.

Yet her mother was determined. Three months became a year. Every day was a new low, or a day to step outside to delight in sunshine.

"I'm really going to beat this," her mother, fondly called GiGi, said.

This relative experienced every moment, lived on-call every day, every hour, not only for her mother, but for her husband and two young children.

As if a general strategizing war, she planned how to tend to her people. Every day, given the changing effects of cancer treatment, found her rescheduling, scheduling, reworking, wrung out dry.

Eighteen months in, fifteen months longer than the doctors gave her, her mother attended a family party. Her blue eyes brightened. Her hair coiffed in her southern way. "I'm going to live," she said. Her doctors had no answer why the cancer had not taken her.

GiGi, as we see in some of our loved ones, ran on belief and strong-will. She lived another several months. Then, her time to pass came.

Karen's life became more spacious. "Honestly, I was relieved the month after mom's passing. I spent time with my kids. I ate dinner out with my husband." Her family cherished the normalcy. "But now, I'm ready for Momma to be back."

Grieving is not the funeral. The celebrations of life are the to-dos that signal a goodbye. A handkerchief waved at a ship's dock to a passenger. Grieving happens later for some of us. We travel from agenda and hankie wave, to shock and ugly cries within months.

We are in life, doing the thing, but internally, we carry hearts that are cried-out, or hearts that hold tears tight. How can anyone understand the pain? We shop the grocery, take the car to an oil change, pick up sweet tea from Mom's favorite hamburger place without mentioning a word of our loss, even though it edges our tongues.

Our lives have been conducted in crisis mode for so many months. Our vernacular has upgraded to understanding creatinine levels and pulse ox's. We minister to our children and find they have learned to make do, or they cling like a sweater in the heat. Everything that was before the illness is gone. Everything that was the illness is gone. We are lost. We slip our sunglasses on at night and remain silent.

We want life back to before the after. We want to go on a beach trip together or to a movie. We are metaphorically stomping our foot for our way, and not getting it. The way we speak to or isolate from our loved ones reveals our child-like hearts.

We want backwards.

Ponder Point Grieving is ongoing. Many of us want to niche the process into five easy steps and be done.

My relative told me how she felt. "It was a vacation, that first month. Then reality set in." She told her mom she wanted her back. Saying the words directed her grief journey. Shaking hands with this idea helps eases the angst of fighting it.

IF YOU BELIEVE LIFE
BEGINS AT CONCEPTION

Every Thursday, my daughter and I stood there, on a width of land I called the "Gaza Strip," outside a pro-choice center. We hoped for an opportunity to talk to the women coming in and offer them support and an ultrasound on the mobile unit. Then, a family event created havoc in our schedule.

As an alternative, I participated in a group prayer call.

"A woman just walked in. She's seventeen-weeks' pregnant," Tim, co-founder of Triad Coalition for Life, said. "Sheri, why don't you pray?"

Don't many of us do that? Pray for another day to breathe this air, to seize the potential of the day?

"Hey, Tim," I said. "Can I pray this one?"

A thirty-year old memory flashed through my mind. I learned I was pregnant at seventeen weeks. Genetics blended with a low BMI due to extreme aerobics suppressed my cycle.

Because of a scratchy throat, I went to Dr. Esserman, my gynecologist, as he was the only doctor I had at twenty-eight.

"You've got strep," he said. Then, he paused. "You're also pregnant."

"What?" I shouted with shock and joy. We had had so many negative tests that I decided to get off the pregnancy rollercoaster. "Really?" I was pregnant.

"Really. An ultrasound in a couple of weeks." He had wanted to make sure before prescribing any medicines. "Let's take care of the strep first."

Two weeks later, the sonogram technician placed the device on my flat stomach. "Sorry for the cold," she said.

"I'm sure it's too early to tell. But I want the sex to be a surprise."

"Well." The screen showed the baby, clear and without a search. "Woman, you're about ready to have this baby," the tech said.

"What do you mean?"

"This child is around nineteen weeks. You need to start planning a baby shower."

I was almost halfway to giving birth.

How quickly it goes by, my mother would say, about my life. How quickly it goes by in our children's lives. Just this summer, my son turned thirty.

What an adventure his life has been. My son's early love of tools has been inherited by his one-year-old son, a toy hammer constantly in hand. My parents spoke with awe on how he disassembled their garage door

"…Observe, the object of the good man's solicitude in life and death is not his body or his estate, but his spirit; this is his jewel, his secret treasure; if this be safe, all is well."

~ Charles H. Spurgeon

one rainy day as a four-year old. He had told my dad and brother at five what they were doing wrong while assembling his new bike.

The boy scout tent trips were part of our family history, one in which we earned the Polar Patch by sleeping outdoors below thirty-two degrees. His prowess displayed in skateboarding, snowboarding, Calculus, and French. The deep talks shared on deep thoughts. The neon orange and blue paint rolled on his teenage basement bedroom.

In the clinic, a mother decided whether her seventeen-week-old baby had the hope of entering this world alive or not.

"God, please let her see past the hardships, past this moment. Help her see her child at two, at four, at sixteen, at thirty. Help her see this child as a blessing. Please." I finished my prayer.

As the sun neared setting, I messaged

Tim. "Is our seventeen-week baby gone?"

My dog and I traversed the pond's dam, checking where the muskrats dug holes causing destruction. The sun lowered behind the trees.

"Yes," he replied.

Ponder Point What might the world miss if a child is not born with a breath?

If you've had an abortion, and are struggling, consider reaching out for help. Local Pregnancy Resource Centers (PRCs) and groups such as lovelife.org and their Restored Life outreach are helping post-abortive women.

THE ELEPHANT IN
THE ROOM

Friend's Point of View

I skipped church to be with a friend, three weeks after her son's death. His German Shepherd greeted me at the door, followed by her husband.

"She's in the kitchen." I scooted away from the massive dog.

Gerri pressed her hands on the oak table, decorated with placemats, to stand. The hug exchanged was tighter and longer than our regular Sunday morning one. My affection needed to make up for words that carried the weight of dust.

After sipping coffee and silence, I picked up a devotional from her stack.

"You're reading this?"

"When I can," Gerri said.

Words rocketed through my head. I weighed and measured each noun and verb for their rightness or wrongness.

"Your flowerbed is beautiful." Gerri's garden bloomed Lazy Susans, coneflowers, and yarrow, an oxymoron of the sadness inside. After fiddling with the coffee cup handle, I straightened the salt and pepper shakers, then folded the gingham napkin.

The elephant needed to be brought up and brought out. Her son Chris was gone. Gerri is lost. I am clueless.

Grieving Friend's Point of View

My friend texted saying she would like to visit. I wanted to stay in bed. Particularly on Sundays. The accident happened Saturday night. Who knows when I'll go back to church?

"Come on over." I did not mean it.

She hugged me too long, reminding me I'd not seen anybody for weeks other than family. A visit must be good for me, if I worried about things like that anymore.

I drink coffee. I eat food. I drink water. My husband Luke slips them in front of me.

"You're reading this?" my friend asked.

When I get out of bed. If I get out of bed. "When I can."

"I don't have any words." She took my hand. "I'm so sorry."

Dale, my son's dog, nudged me. He quit putting his nose on the table, the big lug. Chris must have fed him snacks from his plate. I stroked his bristly hair. My son loved this dog.

"Your son must have loved that dog."

The tears, the never-ending tears, smudged my eyes. "Dale was his baby."

"A big baby." My friend straightened a daisy in the flower arrangement. More cut flowers soon to die.

"I miss him. I keep expecting Chris to come through the door and take his dog home."

"I can't imagine, Gerri."

"He was coming from the lake. His truck ran off the road."

I stirred sugar I could not taste into my coffee.

"He probably was alive for a little bit."

My friend squeezed my hand.

I dabbed my eyes with a tissue from my tenth box. "If it just wouldn't have happened."

Ponder Point If you are the grieving, I wish your loved one was still with you. I'm sorry you have had to put up with those of us bumbling our way through visits. We're trying. It is silly, but we are afraid to bring up your loved one, as if it could hurt even more. Or we talk about our own losses. Either way we veer, our words or lack thereof seem hurtful.

WIPE WHAT?

After Dad passed, Mom's health declined even further. Emotional blows hit deepest, it seems. By this time, we had a rhythm with the caregivers. They did the work of Mom, so we could do the work of being with her. All that changed when Dad passed. Although she had round-the-clock care, Mom needed her children. In between tears of loss over her husband of fifty-five years, she would order us to do things we had not done since our kids were babies. And to our mother, no less. Sickness comes with a lot of wiping. In places, we'd prefer not to go.

The spectrum of grief care for a sick family member is wide, from crying to compression socks, from flower arranging to full-frontals. We learn too much of our loved ones. What do we do with that?

Truly, we have one choice, two alternatives. We develop an attitude. Either run away like a zebra from a lion or recognize the humbling situation for *them* and embrace their need. If we choose stripes, it's far easier, but we miss moments those who espouse to embrace, gain. The laughter at burps, the story long forgotten, a simple meal after a simple prayer, the hand we hold that held us. These are the hardest acts we ever do but are immeasurable in helping a hurting mother through the night, or a mean man to quiet peace, a pained child to smiles.

"Whoever walks in integrity walks securely, but he who makes his ways crooked will be found out."

~ Proverbs 10:9 (ESV)

Ponder Point If you're caring for the parent left behind, and have not walked through a lengthy illness, call in reinforcements. Contact as many friends and groups as possible. Though hard, practice receiving help from others now. Check your attitude. If you're a grump or impatient, you know this about yourself. People have told you. The others who are caring need you to do a swift one-eighty. Be the grown-up. Remember your loved one is grieving too. Be kind to those caregiving. People will walk away from a bad situation.

Check options an organization might offer, such as AMAC, as well as with your parent's insurance agent. An additional policy for help might very well be available.

If this is your first time with insurance, "appeal, appeal, appeal" on your loved one's behalf, according to Jennifer, a pulmonary nurse for many decades. Health-care demands extensive phone calls, as many of you have learned or will.

Set boundaries, or you will burn out, and possibly jeopardize your health. Easy to say, hard to do—prioritize sleep.

The Vultures Are Circling

Alice is a doer. During the day, she handles bookkeeping for a family business. At night and weekend, she works her flower farm's startup. Accounts Receivables and Payables and planting season did not pause for her emergency or heartache. Money, the amoral thing it is, did not account for her grief. Expenses needed paying.

Speaking in weekly meetings is specific to her job. Yet she could barely muster the energy to communicate. Coming home meant blessed silence, working outdoors where she loved. The flow of people visiting after the funeral had trickled to an end. Being alone was a haven.

Out of nowhere, men, single or divorced, came bearing gifts. One brought produce.

He encouraged her to make a sandwich, with spinach, avocado mayonnaise, and the Joe Johnson tomato he had grown. "Toasted multi-grain bread is the secret," he said. "I have an extra panini maker in the car, if you want."

A co-worker mowed the brush growth near her flowers. "I've always been fond of this land. You must really love it." A mentor at work mentioned a remedy to our fatigue. "A foot and back massage will take care of that."

The vultures were circling.

She had trusted these men in normal work situations, but the abnormal acts of kindness put Alice on high alert. Why were they going overboard now? Their motives might have been stellar, but in a time of need, the extra care seemed nothing short of creepy. However, she became wary, with good reason.

She reminded herself of the good men in her life. The owner of the company respected her work excellence. The young father kept her fence lines maintained. The jack-of-all trades down the road, with the large family, installed a much-needed water system. The man who managed her pond only talked about the fish she wanted to add. The handyman installed her new mailbox after a car hit it.

All good men. All there to help. All there to call on in a needed moment. She knew their family stories and had prayed for them through some difficult times. They were safe.

Ponder Point At times, it's difficult to distinguish who are trusted people, particularly after a tragic time. Even texts that are slightly off leads us to doubt people we've previously trusted. To say we're scared of the world is an understatement.

Having to wade through trust issues is hard given the deeper mire to manage. If you have a personality like Alice, where you're concerned about being "mean," choose to delete and ignore any messages received.

Disengage. And disengage again. The message should be loud and clear. If the person persists, block his number from your phone. Don't answer the door.

If it turns out a person was trying to help and you ignored them, the truth will surface. Time will give this person a turn to serve.

Guard your media and never give your phone number out.

ISOLATORS UNITE

Robbie had recounted the story countless times, verbally. He had resorted to cutting and pasting on his phone so he would not have to do it anymore. The normal conversation surrounding the death was over.

He worked at home. His kids were grown. He needed time to himself until he realized the state of his refrigerator. With tears in his eyes he had never told anyone about, Robbie lined up the hardened casseroles that had been stacked three deep in his refrigerator. He laid them out, like a Tim Burton Thanksgiving dinner, crusty, and moldy, and spooky. The cakes, the gloriously homemade cakes that any other time would tempt him, wilted. His wife would never have left the cakes uncovered. It was payback time via the sugar ants that devoured the lemon bundt cake.

She should have been here to do this. She was not.

He struggled with the garbage bag, flipping the plastic around the floor. He opened it wide and scrapped food, all this food, into the lavender scented bags she insisted upon. Not the lemon, not the orange, but the lavender. Because she liked the smell. She always had wanted to go to France and see the lavender. But they'd never gotten around to that, had they?

Robbie had never had many friends. He saw no point, as she was more than enough

"'Hope' is the thing with feathers
That perches in the soul,
And sings the tune without the
words, and never stops—at all."
~ Emily Dickinson

friend for his lifetime. She favored his favorite restaurants and how he liked his coffee. He knew how to wipe the counter down the way she liked after every meal. He knew she liked private spa time in the bathroom at night.

For the second time, he had binge-watched her favorite television shows from Downton Abbey to the M*A*S*H series he had bought her last year for her birthday. He pretended she was still there, bringing her a cup of herbal tea and the Moravian cookies she preferred. It was strange, he knew. But Robbie could not, would not, stop doing that. To do so would be to give into the truth that he was alone. Perhaps their lives had been spent too much that way.

Ponder Point At some point in our grieving lives, we examine our ways with people. Sometimes things we think are perfect are found to be wanting. It's not bad to acknowledge this. However, do not carry this realization alone. Seek a balanced outlook as you look back.

LEARNING YOUR ROLE
IN THE NEW FAMILY
DYNAMICS

When I was a single-digit, after our Saturday evening baths, my cleanliness-determined Mom jumped the rails now and again, allowing us to wander outside to catch lighting bugs. The Queen's Anne's lace, a weed by book standards, but aptly named, drew my attention. These would look perfect on the kitchen table. I would reach deep into the stems and break where the small green branch met the stem, until a collection was gathered.

After slipping into the house before Mom called us in, I would find an appropriate glass to display the weeds. Unlike the professionally created flowers Mom received from Dad, my display was leggy and spread out. But proud I was of my creation.

Then, the middle of the night came. The chiggers burrowed into my skin. In the still of night, Mom applied the stinky and sticky medicine to my reddened patches, halting the progress of the active critters.

I was not deterred. Before picking, I examined the Queen's Anne's lace, pinching off the dots of black and chucking them to the ground. The mystic weed graced our table, and I ended, mostly, my late-night visits to Mom. Soon, Goldenrod, Elderberry, and yellow dandelion were added to my bouquet. I spent hours hunting and picking wild blackberries to bring home to my family. I was the gatherer of the family.

The passing of one or both parents, of a husband, or sibling, makes many of us look at the construction of our families. How they were built, what role we played.

Many of us have done this introspection throughout the years. A death, however, brings insight to the forefront, like chigger bites to skin.

The first year my siblings and I were without parents on earth, I arranged the Christmas get-together, with my sisters' help, and planned the perfect gift for each of Mom and Dad's grandchildren—a bound book from their library collection. One sister suggested a crazy sweater contest, another oversaw the food. The night was full and weighty and outright fun.

Ponder Point Deep sadness accompanies the funeral. Adding the soul-searching of how you fit into the new family dynamic (leader, creative, rebel, peacemaker), and unforeseen emotions complicate. Am I doing this out of habit? Do I have to be the one who cleans the dishes, organizes the to-dos, sends the estate emails out?

As with good and bad memories, be mindful of your thoughts on your role and the feelings behind it. If your other family members come to mind, ponder or write reflections in an assigned notebook for processing familial relations after the flowers die. Shut the cover on these thoughts, until you're ready to approach them. This is a form of rest you need.

A Sad and Funny Story: To be Read Long after the Flowers Die

Thirty years ago, in a move from Miami to a small town in North Carolina, I received a call from a young man we had known in Florida.

"I can't stand this anymore. I need to get away." Chris formulated plans on where he could go, what he could do. He was seventeen.

Having known his family in Miami, I suggested he come up and visit us for a couple of weeks. Chris stayed home to give out the Halloween candy while watching "Star Trek." He played with our young children, while their dad was away often on work. He was legend for not liking vegetables, so he always received carrots on his plate.

The weeks turned to years, until one day, he brought a woman and her children home.

Soon my refrigerator was straightened, and storage was labeled by her hands. My clothes were folded far better than I ever could. The dishes were done. The floor mopped.

Her kids were sweet, but I was raising my own young children. Chris delighted in his adopted family and his new emerging family. I was not ready for the Walton scenario.

"They can't live here," I replied to Chris when he asked. I could not find any food in a perfect refrigerator. I enjoyed sweeping and mopping my own floor at night as a way to close down the day and put another check on the calendar.

"We'll stay in the basement and not be a bother."

Chris was now in his 20s. "You need to move out." A rare moment of good, solid boundaries had popped out of my mouth.

"But…"

"No buts about it. It's time." He packed up, and they left. His life went from bright to dim. His drinking increased into full-blown alcoholism. His job became a shady one, filled with unsavory nighttime activities. Then the calls came.

He was beat up. Hit with a brick. In jail. Weekends were routine calls from the ER.

I spent late hours, when we moved to another house, trying to reach and minister to his heart. He wanted help. But would not accept it from anybody but us. Looking back, he did not concede to our suggestions either. He talked to ease his conscience, having witnessed many sinister acts. He was living a dangerous life.

In his forties, Chris relented. He would go to a rehab program. Yet one rehab became another, became another until we reached six, one in the North Carolina mountains.

"This isn't working," he said. "I'm taking a bus back."

Further and deeper his life meshed with the underside of night.

"I need help."

At a homeschool conference, I stepped outside in worry to take his call. "Chris, I've tried."

Words, horrible words, in a transformed voice that scared the living daylights out of me spewed forth from him.

"Chris," I said, underneath his barrage, "I'm hanging up now."

I called his step-uncle, the only family member Chris responded to and explained what had happened.

"The same with me," this reasoned man reported. "I had to cut ties. It is okay to make a boundary. He is unhealthy."

Stories came to us from other family members who responded to his call on occasion. His alcoholism resulted in more hospital stays and a ravaged esophagus. But Chris kept fighting to live, and live his way, in the clubs and bars.

Finally, one morning I woke to the words in a message: "Chris passed last night."

Pushing the hospital door open, I ventured into his room. "Hi, Chris," I said. The greeting was an attempt at normalcy. His ventilator, still attached, pointed upward like a small trumpet of sorts, as if it too wanted to respond with a sound.

Chris laughing, Chris mad, Chris questioning, Chris rebellious, the six-teen-year old kid we had played church softball with, the Chris who ate all the pea-nut M&Ms, all these pictures filled my mind. But Chris dead? No, he always survived.

"It's been a long ride, hasn't it?" I walked around his bed, unsure what to do, shocked there was no more to do. His black hair, even styled in death, emphasized his Native American heritage. So much Chris should have been, yet never was. Would another year have made a difference?

"…But, being so much too good for earth, Heaven vows to keep him."

~ Ben Jonson

"I hope you made your peace with God." He and I had both been skeptics, until one day I was no longer. Chris had remained mad at God for his childhood all his life.

I messaged my friends who ran a funeral home. "Please pick him up." I left a note on his body, giving further instructions. "I commit his spirit to you, Lord."

The Chris that was the young teen had been long gone. The hope I held for that Chris to return was gone. "I love you."

His mother, whom he wrestled with all the days of his life, and I spoke on his burial. His mother agreed to cremation. My friend and his wife came over, and arrangements were made.

The family here arranged to go to the funeral in Oklahoma. I stayed home. At the funeral, a dispute arose about his ashes. His relatives all wanted them. A compromise was reached. His remains were divided up, with some coming back to North Carolina for his kids. Thankfully, his family resolved the situation.

Until one day, I cleaned the garage. I dug to the back of a shelf and pulled out a box labeled "Cremated Remains."

"What is that?" I shouted to my husband.

"That's Chris."

"Chris?" Chris whose ashes had been properly given to his family? How could there be more?

"Those are for the kids."

"I thought you gave them the box."

"No, I guess I forgot."

My heart pounded. Angst rose to my throat. I'm sure I said it this time. I swore.

"How do you forget something like that? How do you put him in the garage?"

"I'm sorry."

"Well, take him somewhere. Now."

It was halftime for the Panthers, an excellent time for a football interruption. I watched my husband go to his truck.

"I'll get Chris to the kids Monday."

Several years later, I was cleaning my husband's truck that I had started driving, since his Parkinson's had parked him. I flipped up the seat. A box had been hidden

there. Chris had been driving around with me for six months. I am sure I interrupted the Panthers again.

Chris was moved back to the garage, my husband tasked with the instructions of dealing with him. "I mean it, this time." End of story. My garage was now clean.

After the tree almost killed me and we moved to a farm, my daughter-in-heart asked to organize the move of the house, as an act of love.

For one who does not like her food lined up in the fridge and labeled, this was a godsend.

During the move, she came to me with a box. "What is this?"

It could not be, but it was. I was glad the cable had been turned off. My husband could hear me loud and clear.

Chris was put back on the shelf that was labeled for the movers to NOT MOVE.

Much unpacking occurred. My adult children do as they always do, rally to the parents to help, being the amazing children that they are.

We finally made it to the boxes labeled

"Garage." Do I need to say what I found and what I said?

That Thanksgiving, we reminisced about Chris, who disliked Thanksgiving, given his heritage, and by now, the box had entered family lore.

I had his children over several days later for dinner, specifically to give them their father's remains. We enjoyed the reunion so much that all thoughts of the box were forgotten.

"Come get Chris," I tell one of my sons. "His kids need to do this before Kayla goes back to school." They planned on sprinkling their father somewhere serene and mountainous.

The Panthers are no longer watched at my home. The cable is gone. The family is scattered, even more so given the past two years.

Life we are gifted, three, maybe four generations, is full of peaks and valleys, my grandmother used to say, then my mother, now me. Peaks and valleys. So many peaks and valleys.

The pond reflects the trees. A bass ripples the water. The sugar maple branch hangs to the ground. I need to cut that down today. There's nobody left to ask.

Perhaps Chris will end up at the farm after all, the wind lifting him to root and rest, at last.

Ponder Point As hard as it is, walking with someone in their life's journey to the end, and in this case even after, is the most important act we can do. Whether they follow a hard road or a good path, we have to assert boundaries. This does not negate or lessen our support of them. If anything, boundaries heighten relationships and bring balance to our lives, particularly when loving troubled people. After the walk is said and done, seek peace and comfort in having known this person and having lived out your lives together.

DEAR ONES

Maple leaves grace the ground. The hummingbirds have migrated to a warmer climate. I've stacked firewood for the upcoming winter. Thanksgiving is but days away. My shopping list has started, but the graciousness of my adult children, and their love of cooking, will not only complete, but celebrate the day.

Four years ago, after almost a decade and a half of my mom's cancer battle, I was called home. It was surprising. My mother always rallied for Thanksgiving, then Christmas, if only to wear the red sweater that highlighted her blue eyes and big smile. Half-expecting her to rebound by the time I was there, since my siblings and I had been called home multiple times, I knew the drill. I delighted in the three-hour drive of glorious mountains, and knew the good stops for coffee and snacks, when the cell signal would drop, even when I would tire of news radio and switch to 70s rock.

By the time I got to my mother, her speech was incoherent, but she spoke to me, reams of words I couldn't understand. Not knowing what to do, I nodded my head, and would bring up regular concerns she had this time of year. Theresa was decorating the tree. Instead of having to order gifts, why didn't Mom give books from my parents' collection to her grandchildren? This seemed to enliven my mother, as she loved nothing more than paring down the items in her house. "I'd rather see you kids get things now and enjoy them while I'm still here," my mother often said as if her motto.

Standing by her side, my siblings and I took turns visiting. Mom loved having her children about her. My brother tweaked her nose like he did every time he saw her. My sister rubbed her hands. My other brother leaned in for a kiss.

"She was speaking so well last night," my sister said. My mother stared at me so intensely, as if trying to communicate something, but I could not read her thoughts, a regret I have to this day.

My siblings all lived in town. Being the lone out-of-towner, I worried about the twenty-two family members coming to my house. Privately, the doctor told me Mom had several days to go before her heart would give out. "Go home. Get your dinner in order, then come back," she said. For the first time in twelve years, I listened to a doctor's prediction. My brothers and sister gave me their blessing.

"Mom, I'm going to run home and get the tables ready, then come back." My children and their spouses, who always rallied for the family's needs, would be able to cook, feast

"But people themselves alter so much, that there is something new to be observed in them forever."

~ Jane Austen, *Pride and Prejudice*

and pull off this most special dinner with excellence. I could do what I needed in a snap without Mom missing me.

At home, having brought my daughters' their favorite Chinese food, we gathered around the table, and I listened to their lives. As soon as we finished, my phone buzzed. My sister's face popped up on the screen, and I knew.

"She's gone, sweetie." My sister spoke other words to me, then held the phone to Mom's ear, just as she had Dad's. "I love you, Momma." Never would I sleep next to her again, the habit begun on the night my father passed, so she wouldn't be alone. Never would Mom wear the vibrant St. John suits she so loved. But free of that hated wheelchair, she was.

I went where I had two years earlier when my father had died, years earlier when Chuck had passed, then his wife, Susan. The side porch was my refuge from the storm, my quiet place, where the dogwood berries had turned red, and the old oak's trunk, so many feet wide, had long been veined by honeybees. Here, out in nature, I sobbed, as I had with the others, as I had listening to so many heartbreaks, this place where the sunrise greeted me only after the leaves fell.

My mother was gone. My father was gone. It's the closest I've come to feeling orphaned, so unlike the hardships my adopted daughters experienced, but a deep wrenching, all the same. My parents were the people on this planet who had known me my entire life. Through the sweet times and bad ones, they encouraged, blessed, raised a whole lot of concerns because this rebellious one needed them, and sent me roses once on my birthday when I was in college, and a poinsettia, and smoked salmon and trout every year. I did plenty wrong and right, as they did, yet I was their people, part of the whole family story that happens when a Fleenor/Ramey meets a Leonard/Kaylor.

As I plan for this year's Thanksgiving, I recognize the anniversaries of their passing, and wish so badly I could kiss their cheeks one more time, sit on the back porch with my dad and talk cattle and politics, watch Mom rearrange her drawers for the umpteenth time. Many times, I have, as one almost six decades old, wanted my parents to lean on, to know someone more adult than I still parented me. Other days, I am so wrapped in living that their passing isn't on my radar. And I feel no guilt. Just a certain peace that life is moving forward, to that moment in time when my children are the oldest generation.

My kids do not like to talk about that, but talk I do. (Because who can stop a train?) They know the location of the important documents. I have made arrangements for my funeral. Since life circumstances have changed, I've updated my will. I've familiarized my adult children with the paperwork of passing, as best I can. It is a huge process, whether your estate is an apartment or castle.

Educate your children about your life goals and desire to leave a legacy of moral gains, not just financial ones. There is still so much to do, but starting the task is far better than leaving your children grieving through unknown paperwork and possessions.

If your children are minors, I beg you to get a will and assign the proper people to care for them. Skip a dinner out once a month and purchase life insurance. Write individual letters to your little ones telling them the hopes and dreams you hope for their lives. Show wise discipline, but always show them love.

Consider starting a collection for them, and giving one piece a year to your young, so that years after you're gone, they have memorable tokens of your love. My mother-in-law bought all her grandchildren Christmas ornaments. An uncle gifted a young man I know a gold coin every year. Writing in a journal periodically is simple, inexpensive, and priceless.

The best planning we can do happens around a table with takeout, or turkey, where differences might arise, but love overrides. Passing down the family stories, the family values, the great moments of laughter are the best of legacies. My hope and prayer for you all is that a legacy of love becomes your preeminent concern.

God's Speed, Dear Ones. You are not alone.

Reading Recommendations

Entrusted: Building a Legacy That Lasts, David R. York and Andrew L. Howell

The Total Money Makeover, Dave Ramsey

Rich Dad, Poor Dad, Robert T. Kiyosaki

Wealth, Stuart E. Lucas

Chaos Can't, Allen Arnold

How to Live through a Bad Day, Jack W. Hayford

Psalms and Proverbs, the *Bible*

Extraordinary Hospitality for Ordinary Christians, Victoria Duerstock

Redeeming Your Time, Jordan Raynor

A Guide for Grown-ups, Antoine de Saint-Exupery

Only the Paranoid Survive, Andrew S. Grove

The Chronicles of Narnia, the series, C.S. Lewis

Amusing Ourselves to Death, Neil Postman

The Giving Tree, Shel Silverstein

Quotation References

Page 2   C.S. Lewis, *A Grief Observed*, Seabury Press, 1961.ll

Page 5   Frances Hodgson Burnett, *The Secret Garden*, Frederick A. Stokes, 1911.

Page 15   J.R.R. Tolkien, *The Fellowship of the Ring*, Allen & Unwin, 1968.

Page 24   https://www.poetryfoundation.org/poems/44644/a-psalm-of-life

Page 28   Antoine de Saint-Exupery, A Guide for Grown-ups, Houghton Mifflin Hardcourt, 2002.

Page 36   https://www.blueletterbible.org/Comm/murray_andrew/surrender/surrender02.cfm

Page 54   https://archive.spurgeon.org/treasury/ps130.php

Page 56   L.B. Cowman, *Streams in the Desert*, Zondervan, 2006.

Page 61   Siv Ashley, *A Teenager's Survival: The Siv Ashley Story*, Paws and Claws Publishing Service LLC, 2013.

Page 82   C.S. Lewis, *The Last Battle*, The Bodley Head, 1956.

Page 84   https://thedewdrop.org/2019/08/21/let-us-be-contented-winston-churchill/

Page 96   https://www.blueletterbible.org/Comm/mcgee_j_vernon/eBooks/what-do-you-do/what-do-you-do-with-your-fears.cfm

Page 99   L.B. Cowman, *Streams in the Desert*, Zondervan, 2006.

Page 115   https://archive.spurgeon.org/treasury/ps031.php

Page 123   https://www.poetryfoundation.org/poems/42889/hope-is-the-thing-with-feathers-314

Page 129   https://www.poetryfoundation.org/poems/44453/an-epitaph-on-sp

Page 133   Jane Austen, *Pride and Prejudice*, T. Egerton, Whitehall, 1813.

Acknowledgments

The dairy-free icing on the gluten-free cake for me after reading a book is rejoicing in all those whom the writer thanks. How to list a plethora of people?

Writing *After the Flowers Die* was only possible because of all the people who shared their lives with me, and I with them. Loss overshadows our lives, but each of you show me the spirit of life that moves you forward. What inspiration and beauty you bring to the world in the deep hurts. Peace abound to you, dear ones.

Several years ago, a woman coached me about my world. She listened to my saga, suggested work habits and how to build platform, then one day, counseled which book idea I should focus on. Victoria Duerstock, what a wild ride! My love to your family.

A gracious plenty to the most excellent team at End Game Press, both behind the scenes and the other EGP authors, whom I've gleaned much. Hope, you are most aptly named.

Kudos for reading rough words and being ever so encouraging and enthusiastic, Laura Smith, David Lawrence and Stephanie Scearce.

Much respect and appreciation to those who've shepherded this straying heart back home, Joel Smith, Dan Shoaf, Justin Bingham, Robert Hefner and Roger Bailey.

Ditto to the many professionals who've arranged my passing to be as smooth a transition to my loved ones as possible, including the infinite Planner of planners, the Lord God Almighty, maker of heaven and earth.

Thanks to the wonders of Word Weavers International (go, Word Weavers Piedmont Triad!), Serious Writer Club, Redeeming Your Time CC, #HealthyFaith, Building Platform 101, Writers Chat, and the families of Electro-Mechanical Corporation.

The Lord has blessed me with a priceless sisterhood. Thanks to you all for traveling the long road with me, including the 5Gs (Becky, JSho, Laura and Shanda), the Ripple Effect

(BriJ, Tracie, Maribeth, Barbara, Robin, Sebrina and Rachael), the women of Wellspring Community and Pleasant Garden Baptist Churches, Dyanne B., and grand Poet friend, Tina Barr. The invaluable mentors of my younger daughters, Genevieve Traversy and Celia Murillo, and our travel-meister and deep roots' conversationalist, Anna Gray Smith. Thanks also to the memories and new ones, dear cousins. Edie Melson and DiAnn Mills, O sweet and true ones, no words. There are so many more sisters. I love you all.

Thank you to my farm people, who guide the land into a vision of provision and community. To the grand ole oak that fell on our house, thus moving us to the land of my heart. To the city of Bristol, its state line, bluegrass history and music that feeds my soul. And yes, Shanda, our Jimmy Cliff and the *Journey*.

As mentioned in the beginning, my brothers and sister. Thank you for traversing life with me as the 4Rs. Overwhelming love too to your spouses, Carol, Lee and Kim, and my nieces and nephews.

*Always on my mind and in my heart are my precious, delightfully creative children and their loves, my grands and those generations yet to be. Your remarkable grace and love astound me. You all are a hoot and my best blessings, through dinners to vacations, to the everyday and the hard, you each and every one shine. I love you with all the excellent adjectives in the 1828 Webster's Dictionary.

But above all, my everlasting gratitude to He who brought me out of darkness and into His marvelous light. Glory be to the One True God. Glory!

About the Author

RENEE LEONARD KENNEDY, as many writers do, remembers writing as one of her first memories. After decades of wandering, she came back to words, first in the white space of her Bible, then in stories and ideas.

She thanks God for family, friends, acquaintances, once-in-a-lifetime encounters, and books.

Writing and reading, working her farm, and with her adult kids to further their entrepreneurial spirits blesses her heart. Gathering around the table or fire pit with loved ones is her life's pinnacle.

Renee is active with Triad Coalition for Life, Save the Storks, Sister Keepers and Pleasant Garden Baptist Church. She is a new board member to The Oaks Community, a non-profit organization with a focus on mental health and wellness, serving the Piedmont Triad and partners nationwide (www.theoakscommunity.org).

The first and last word on her is that she's a follower of Jesus Christ.